CRIMES OF GENDER

VIOLENCE AGAINST WOMEN

IDEAS in CONFLICT

Gary E. McCuen

GEM
GARY McCUEN
publications inc.

411 Mallalieu Drive
Hudson, WI 54016
Phone (715) 386-7113

Illustrations and Photo Credits

Amnesty International 135, Jim Borgman 92, Carol & Simpson 61, 77, 105, David Horsey 111, Craig MacIntosh 100, Oxfam America 40, Steve Sack 83, 96, David Seavey 125, Eddie Thomas 11, Richard Wright 53, 57

publications inc.

© 1994 by Gary E. McCuen Publications, Inc.
411 Mallalieu Drive, Hudson, Wisconsin 54016

(715) 386-7113

International Standard Book Number
ISBN 0-86596-092-5
Printed in the United States of America

CONTENTS

Ideas in Conflict   6

Chapter 1 **GLOBAL VIOLENCE AGAINST WOMEN: AN OVERVIEW**

1. BOSNIAN HORROR: THE RAPE   9
   AND GENOCIDE
   Amnesty Action

2. MUTILATION OF FEMALE GENITALIA   14
   Janie Hampton

3. LITTLE GIRLS DYING: FEMALE INFANTICIDE   20
   IN CHINA AND INDIA
   Jo McGowan

4. WOMEN IN INDIA FACE ABUSE FROM BIRTH   24
   Jim Landers

5. SEXUAL SLAVERY IN THAILAND   30
   Gayle Reaves

6. CHILDBIRTH AND DEATH IN POOR NATIONS   35
   Jodi L. Jacobson

7. WOMEN BEAR THE BRUNT OF POVERTY   39
   Oxfam America

8. WOMEN AND VIOLENCE IN NATIVE CULTURES   43
   Cultural Survival Quarterly

9. STDs: THE OTHER EPIDEMIC   46
   Jodi L. Jacobson

10. MASSIVE VIOLENCE IN AMERICA   52
    The Unforgettable Fire

11. RAPE IN AMERICA   55
    The National Women's Study

12. BATTERED WOMEN   59
    Dale H. Robinson

EXAMINING SEXIST STEREOTYPES   64
Reasoning Skill Activity

Chapter 2 **GENDER BASED CRIME AND
THE VIOLENCE AGAINST WOMEN ACT**

13. THE RIGHT RESPONSE TO RAPE   67
    Senate Judiciary Committee

14. THE WRONG RESPONSE TO RAPE   74
    Neil Gilbert

15. RAPE IS A GENDER BASED CRIME   80
    Kristian Miccio

16. RAPE IS NOT GENDER BASED   85
    Alan H. Levy

17. FEMINISTS ARE TO BLAME FOR   90
    ANTI-WOMEN VIOLENCE
    Don Feder

18. MEN ARE RESPONSIBLE FOR   94
    GENDER VIOLENCE
    Susan J. Berkson

INTERPRETING EDITORIAL CARTOONS   99
    Reasoning Skill Activity

Chapter 3 **CONTROLLING SEXUAL OFFENDERS**

19. SEXUAL PREDATORS AND PRISON   102
    TERMS: AN OVERVIEW
    Bill Richards

20. TREATING SEXUAL OFFENDERS: 109
    THE POINT
    Andrew Vachss

21. TREATING SEXUAL OFFENDERS: 114
    THE COUNTERPOINT
    Task Force on Sexual Violence

22. AN ARGUMENT AGAINST PREVENTIVE   119
    DETENTION
    Minnesota Civil Liberties Union

23. IN SUPPORT OF PREVENTIVE DETENTION   123
    State of Minnesota

Chapter 4 INTERNATIONAL HUMAN RIGHTS
           ABUSES AGAINST WOMEN

24. IN SUPPORT OF THE CONVENTION TO   132
    ELIMINATE DISCRIMINATION AGAINST
    WOMEN
    Amnesty International

25. THE CONVENTION VIOLATES THE U.S.   139
    CONSTITUTION
    Ellen Smith

26. U.S. POLICY AND GLOBAL RIGHTS FOR   144
    WOMEN: POINTS AND COUNTERPOINTS
    Jackie Wolcott vs Gordon R. Chapman

RECOGNIZING AUTHOR'S POINT OF VIEW   149
    Reasoning Skill Activity

BIBLIOGRAPHY: Useful Research Materials   151

REASONING SKILL DEVELOPMENT

These activities may be used as individualized study guides for students in libraries and resource centers or as discussion catalysts in small group and classroom discussions.

1. Examining SEXIST STEREOTYPES   64

2. Interpreting EDITORIAL CARTOONS   99

3. What Is SEX BIAS?   128

4. Recognizing AUTHOR'S POINT OF VIEW   149

IDEAS in CONFLICT

This series features ideas in conflict on political, social, and moral issues. It presents counterpoints, debates, opinions, commentary, and analysis for use in libraries and classrooms. Each title in the series uses one or more of the following basic elements:

Introductions *that present an issue overview giving historic background and/or a description of the controversy.*

Counterpoints *and debates carefully chosen from publications, books, and position papers on the political right and left to help librarians and teachers respond to requests that treatment of public issues be fair and balanced.*

Symposiums *and forums that go beyond debates that can polarize and oversimplify. These present commentary from across the political spectrum that reflect how complex issues attract many shades of opinion.*

A **global** *emphasis with foreign perspectives and surveys on various moral questions and political issues that will help readers to place subject matter in a less culture-bound and ethnocentric frame of reference. In an ever-shrinking and interdependent world, understanding and cooperation are essential. Many issues are global in nature and can be effectively dealt with only by common efforts and international understanding.*

Reasoning skill *study guides and discussion activities provide ready-made tools for helping with critical reading and evaluation of content. The guides and activities deal with one or more of the following:*

RECOGNIZING AUTHOR'S POINT OF VIEW

INTERPRETING EDITORIAL CARTOONS

VALUES IN CONFLICT

WHAT IS EDITORIAL BIAS?

WHAT IS SEX BIAS?

WHAT IS POLITICAL BIAS?

WHAT IS ETHNOCENTRIC BIAS?

WHAT IS RACE BIAS?

WHAT IS RELIGIOUS BIAS?

From across **the political spectrum** *varied sources are presented for research projects and classroom discussions. Diverse opinions in the series come from magazines, newspapers, syndicated columnists, books, political speeches, foreign nations, and position papers by corporations and nonprofit institutions.*

About the Editor

Gary E. McCuen is an editor and publisher of anthologies for public libraries and curriculum materials for schools. Over the past years his publications have specialized in social, moral and political conflict. They include books, pamphlets, cassettes, tabloids, filmstrips and simulation games, many of them designed from his curriculums during 11 years of teaching junior and senior high school social studies. At present he is the editor and publisher of the *Ideas in Conflict* series and the *Editorial Forum* series.

CHAPTER 1

GLOBAL VIOLENCE AGAINST WOMEN: AN OVERVIEW

1. BOSNIAN HORROR: THE RAPE AND GENOCIDE 9
   Amnesty Action

2. MUTILATION OF FEMALE GENITALIA 14
   Janie Hampton

3. LITTLE GIRLS DYING: FEMALE INFANTICIDE 20
   IN CHINA AND INDIA
   Jo McGowan

4. WOMEN IN INDIA FACE ABUSE FROM BIRTH 24
   Jim Landers

5. SEXUAL SLAVERY IN THAILAND 30
   Gayle Reaves

6. CHILDBIRTH AND DEATH IN POOR NATIONS 35
   Jodi L. Jacobson

7. WOMEN BEAR THE BRUNT OF POVERTY 39
   Oxfam America

8. WOMEN AND VIOLENCE IN NATIVE CULTURES 43
   Cultural Survival Quarterly

9. STDs: THE OTHER EPIDEMIC 46
   Jodi L. Jacobson

10. MASSIVE VIOLENCE IN AMERICA 52
    The Unforgettable Fire

11. RAPE IN AMERICA 55
    The National Women's Study

12. BATTERED WOMEN 59
    Dale H. Robinson

EXAMINING SEXIST STEREOTYPES 64
Reasoning Skill Activity

1 GLOBAL VIOLENCE AGAINST WOMEN: AN OVERVIEW

BOSNIAN HORROR: THE RAPE AND GENOCIDE

Amnesty Action

The following article is excerpted from an Amnesty International USA *publication* Amnesty Action. *Amnesty International is an organization devoted to promoting basic human rights.*

Points to Consider:

1. Describe how sexual abuse in Bosnia-Herzegovina is part of a pattern of ethnic repression.

2. What indication is there that sexual abuse is carried out in an organized systematic way?

3. What action is proposed by Amnesty International?

"Women Under the Gun," **Amnesty Action**, Spring, 1993. Reprinted by permission.

Sexual abuse has been widespread and sometimes systematic.

Rape is one of the oldest and most common forms of degradation visited upon women when armed men are given license to enforce their will at gunpoint. And in the ruptured republics that once comprised Yugoslavia, the rule of law has long been supplanted by the rule of guns.

Whatever ethnic, religious or political differences may divide them, all women share a common fear in Bosnia-Herzegovina today. Rape. In November, an Amnesty International fact-finding mission returned from the Balkans with confirmation that rape has become an all too common feature of the ugly civil conflict raging there — with all sides engaging in the practice.

"Sexual abuse has been widespread and sometimes systematic," says Amnesty. "It seems to fit into the pattern of ethnic repression which has tragically characterized this war. In fact, women have sometimes been taken captive by soldiers specifically to be raped."

TWO REPORTS

Amnesty released two reports based on information gleaned during its latest mission: (Bosnia-Herzegovina: Rape and Sexual Abuse by Armed Forces) and (Bosnia-Herzegovina: A Wound in the Soul). The second report contains the daily diary of a Muslim man who witnessed seven months of brutality in one town in Bosnia-Herzegovina. Amnesty's latest mission was the second the organization has dispatched to the region within the last six months.

"While forces from all sides in the conflict have raped women, and women from all backgrounds have become victims, Muslim women, in particular, have been the chief victims at the hands of Serbian armed factions," says Amnesty.

ORGANIZED RAPE

Amnesty International believes that the rape and sexual abuse of women by Serbian forces throughout Bosnia Herzegovina has been carried out in an organized and systematic way, with the deliberate detention of women for sexual assault part of a wider pattern of terrorism and intimidation against the Muslim and Croat communities. The intimidation is apparently intended to force Muslims to flee or to leave compliantly when evicted from their homes.

Illustration by Eddie Thomas. Reprinted with permission of the **Star Tribune**, Minneapolis.

"Whether rape has been explicitly singled out by political and military leaders as a weapon against their opponents remains open to question," says Amnesty. "What is clear is that so far effective measures have rarely, if ever, been taken against such abuses and that, in practice, local political and military officers must have had knowledge of and generally condoned it."

While many women have been randomly raped by soldiers simply passing through town, others have been picked up and taken to detention centers and hotels (now used as military brothels) where they have been repeatedly raped by soldiers.

In one case, a 17-year-old Muslim girl told a doctor that Serbian soldiers took her and other women from her village to some huts in the woods nearby. She said that they held her there for three months along with 23 other women. She was among 12 women who were repeatedly raped in front of the other women. When the other women tried to intervene, she said, they were beaten by the soldiers.

Stories like hers are now beginning to be substantiated by Serbian soldiers who have themselves taken part in the abuse. A 21-year-old Bosnian Serb soldier, captured by Bosnian Government forces in 1992, confessed to and said he witnessed a number of gross human rights abuses.

The young soldier told a correspondent of the *New York Times* that he had personally been involved in the rape and murder of eight women in or around a small motel in Vogosca, north of Sarajevo. The soldier said a military commander controlling the premises had, in fact, encouraged the soldiers to "take the women" and not return them.

NOT ONLY MUSLIM WOMEN

But it is not only Muslim women who are being targeted. A 28-year-old Serbian nurse from Brcko told a Belgrade newspaper that she had been detained, raped and beaten by Croatian forces in Slavonski Brod. The woman said she was returning from a visit to Germany when she was stopped by Croat police near Sisak in Croatia in January 1992. She was ordered off the bus along with three other women, all of Serbian nationality.

The nurse reported she was taken to a detention camp in an oil refinery at Slavonski Brod on the border with Bosnia-Herzegovina. She said she was repeatedly raped as were the other women held there. She was pregnant by the time she was transferred to another detention center in a school in Odzak. The woman ultimately bought her way out of captivity with foreign currency she had hidden in her clothing.

"When I first read our report it caused me to start shaking with rage," says Leslie Watson-Davis, Chair of Amnesty International

BOSNIAN HORROR

What is happening in Bosnia and Herzegovina to Muslim and Croatian women seems unprecedented in the history of war crimes.

Women are raped by Serbian soldiers in an organized and systematic way, as a planned crime to destroy a whole Muslim population, to destroy a society's cultural, traditional and religious integrity.

The numbers are chilling: The Ministry of Interior of Bosnia and Herzegovina estimated that 50,000 women and girls had been raped and many impregnated on purpose.

Slavenka Drakulic, **New York Times**, December 1992

USA's Women and Human Rights Steering Committee. Last year Amnesty International issued a detailed report on human rights abuses suffered by women world wide.

"As a woman it stirs something deep inside me. Unfortunately what's going on in Yugoslavia today is not atypical. Rape is a particular form of abuse visited on women that is all too common throughout the world in areas of military conflict. That's why it is important that Amnesty be out in the lead on this issue. Rape is torture. We all need to be calling on our own representatives and our U.N. delegates to take action. We need to let those responsible know that we are watching and we are marking down everything that they do and they will be held responsible."

"Our immediate objective is to stop the rape and other tortures currently being suffered by women and girls in Bosnia-Herzegovina," says Jack Rendler, AIUSA's Campaign Director. "Our long-term goal is to secure universal acceptance of the need to respect and protect the basic human rights of women throughout the world."

2 GLOBAL VIOLENCE AGAINST WOMEN: AN OVERVIEW

MUTILATION OF FEMALE GENITALIA

Janie Hampton

Janie Hampton is a free-lance writer specializing in women's health issues. The following article appeared in the New Internationalist, *a magazine with a focus on world problems and global issues.*

Points to Consider:

1. Analyze why female genital mutilation is practiced.

2. What are short-term and long-term physical effects of the muti-lation?

3. Discuss the implications of eliminating a cultural practice.

4. Contrast the probable effectiveness of legal solutions vs educa-tion in ending mutilation.

Janie Hampton, "Going to Grannie's," **New Internationalist**, February, 1993. Reprinted by permission.

The extreme form, infibulation, involves cutting off both clitoris and labia minora, and scraping out the flesh inside the labia majora.

It now took a quarter of an hour for her to pee. Her menstrual periods lasted ten days. She was incapacitated by cramps lasting nearly half the month. There were premenstrual cramps: cramps caused by the near impossibility of flow passing through so tiny an aperture as M'Lissa had left after fastening together the raw sides of Tashi's vagina with a couple of thorns and inserting a straw so that in healing, the traumatized flesh might not grow together, shutting the opening completely; cramps caused by the residual flow that could not find its way out, was not reabsorbed into her body and had nowhere to go. There was the odor, too, of soured blood, which no amount of scrubbing ever washed off.

The passage is fictional. It might well be fact. It comes from *Possessing the Secret of Joy*, a new novel by Alice Walker. The black American feminist who writes with candor about culture-charged areas of female lives has chosen to explore the practice whereby millions of African girls arrive at womanhood with their clitoris wholly or partly cut out. She has described a young woman's desire, later regretted, to become a full member of her tribe by subjecting herself to genital mutilation. Walker has faced up to the attack that, as an American woman, she has no right to oppose African culture.

Walker's renown has helped to raise consciousness about a process many African girls look forward to — inexplicably in Western eyes — as their rebirth as a mature woman.

FEMALE CIRCUMCISION

"Female circumcision," as it is euphemistically called, comes in different degrees of severity. In the mildest form, sunna, the hood of a girl's clitoris is cut off. The most common form is total excision — clitoridectomy. The extreme form, infibulation, involves cutting off both clitoris and labia minora, and scraping out the flesh inside the labia majora. The vulva is sewn together or pinned with thorns, leaving a very small aperture. In the village setting, there is no anesthetic, beyond sitting in a cold stream. The operation is carried out by older women on girls aged from a few months to puberty depending on local custom. Their legs are tied until the wound has healed.

The World Health Organization (WHO) estimates that 90 million girls and women alive today have endured one or the other procedure, and that two million more girls do so each year. Most are in Sahelian Africa, especially Sudan, Somalia and Mali; but girls in Arab States and parts of Asia are also mutilated in this way. In Europe and North America some immigrant families persist in the practice, either finding willing doctors or sending their unsuspecting daughters home in the school holidays.

The campaign against female genital mutilation began in earnest around 12 years ago. Originally much of the impetus came from Western feminists, but African women have become increasingly active and now predominate. The subject is extremely sensitive not only because it concerns women's sexuality in so acute a way but because to outsiders the shocking nature of a custom taken for granted in so many traditional African societies represents as barbarous both African men and the mothers and "grannies" who insist upon and perform the operation.

Whatever the desire to respect other people's cultures, how can such a practice be condoned? More and more African women insist that it cannot. "I love my culture," says Hadijah Ahmed of the African Women's Welfare Group, "but it is not this. This is torture hiding behind culture. Children have no voice — adult women must speak out to protect them."

MUTILATION

Why is genital mutilation performed on African girls? It is seen as part of the ritual passage from childhood to adulthood, carried out at the climax of various rites performed to signify that girls are ready to be passed on from the ownership of a father to that of a husband. Without the hallmark of "circumcision", the girl could not find a husband or be treated as a full member of adult society.

The practice, then, is the female counterpart of male coming-of-age rituals. But to this, Efua Dorkenoo, director of the Foundation for Women's Health, Research and Development (FORWARD) responds: "This is far worse than male circumcision, both at the time and in long-term effects. This can only be described as mutilation."

The practice awesomely exemplifies men's fear of women's sexuality. Cut and restitched, the girl's genital area is under control. If her virginity is lost, and the fleshly seal breached, it will be obvious.

LIKE A BURNING FLAME

It was like a burning flame, and I screamed. My mother held my head so that I could not move it; my aunt caught hold of my right arm, and my grandmother took charge of my left. Two strange women who I had not seen before tried to keep me from moving my thighs by pushing them as far apart as possible. The daya sat between these two women, holding a sharp razor in her hand which she used to cut off the clitoris. I was scared and suffered such great pain that I lost consciousness at the flame that seemed to sear me through and through.

— Anonymous Egyptian woman

Quoted in "The Hidden Face of Eve," by Nawal El Saadawi (Zed Press, 1980)

Men are guaranteed virgins who are unlikely to stray. Sex for the future woman is to be a duty, not a pleasure.

To some eyes, the results of genital reconstruction are appealing, an improvement on the wet, lumpy natural female genitals, source of uncontrollable desires. After thousands of years aesthetic view conforms with deeply embedded attitudes about sex, virginity and marriage. After the operation a girl is smooth, dry and in control of her body.

Many of the peoples who practice infibulation come from remote desert areas and cling to ancient ways. They fear that an end to the practice would lead to an epidemic of premarital and extramarital sex. The urban lifestyle is seen as shockingly degenerate and immoral. This perception causes many parents to reaffirm the decision to have their daughters "done" even when they are far from home, and the notion that they cannot otherwise find husbands or be socially accepted is hard to sustain. Some believe that there is a religious obligation to operate on their daughters, though no established religion endorses this.

HEALTH EFFECTS

Apart from the risks to the girl from the actual operation — hemorrhage, tetanus, septicemia, damaged urinary tract, severe pain, psychological shock, even death — the health effects last a lifetime. Infections due to trapped urine or menstrual blood may lead to infertility. Sex may be painful, birth complicated. Dr. Mary

McCaffery, a London obstetrician, was shocked when she saw her first infibulated pregnant woman. "Somehow a baby had to get out of a tiny hole surrounded by scar tissue. Internal examination is impossible." McCaffery operates to remove scar tissue several weeks before the birth. "Even with a general anesthetic some of the women scream when their genitals are touched. The pain is not just physical — it goes very, very deep and will be with them forever."

In the Western world, steps have been taken to outlaw female genital mutilation where it is practiced among immigrant groups. In Canada the practice violates the criminal code and a practitioner can get up to 14 years' imprisonment; parents, up to 10 years for criminal negligence. In 1985, it was made explicitly illegal in Britain, and a child at risk can be put on the child protection register.

However, in the Netherlands the Minister of Health has been asked to make the practice allowable in Dutch hospitals. "The proposers believe that this is safer than illegal operations, and non-racist," said Berhane Ras-Work, President of the Inter-African Committee (IAC) Against Harmful Traditional Practices. "But this would put our work back to the beginning." The WHO concurs. "To permit the operation in the hygienic conditions of hospitals grants it medical acceptance and effectively legalizes it," says Dr. Liela Mehra.

But the main efforts to prevent daughters from "going to grannie's" must take place in the countries concerned. The leading international organization in this context is the IAC which now has member groups in 23 African countries. The IAC avoids value judgments, pointing instead to the physical and psychological health damage to girls and women. The groups hold workshops and promote training among village midwives — guardians of women's reproductive health in much of Africa.

EDUCATION

Education, especially of women, is the single most important factor in persuading parents to abandon the practice. Not only can education impart health dangers, but it provides an alternative context in which previous notions about feminine sexuality and marital responsibility can be upheld. Traditionalists need to learn that virginity is prized in many societies, but does not require that clitoridectomy be performed as a sanction.

Progress is slow, but it is happening. In Burkino Faso, for example, a national committee of politicians and popular associations is active. Prison sentences of up to 10 years are meted out to dissuade practitioners. A Burkinabe film has been made: "My Daughter Has Not Been Excised." "Many mothers are now proud to show us their daughters who have not been mutilated,"says Ras-Work. "The practice is definitely decreasing. With effort it should eventually die out."

3   GLOBAL VIOLENCE AGAINST WOMEN: AN OVERVIEW

LITTLE GIRLS DYING: FEMALE INFANTICIDE IN CHINA AND INDIA

Jo McGowan

Jo McGowan lives in India and is a regular contributor to Commonweal, *a Catholic publication of social and religious commentary, based in New York City.*

Points to Consider:

1. Analyze the Chinese sex ratio of 118.5 newborn boys for 100 girls.

2. Examine the moral difference between abortion and infanticide.

3. What role does modern technology play in sex selection?

4. Compare / contrast the birth options of Chinese women with the options of Americans.

Jo McGowan, "Little Girls Dying," **Commonweal**, August 9, 1991. Reprinted by permission.

*In both countries, female infanticide is an ancient and,
in many areas, still thriving practice.*

When we named our adopted daughter Moy Moy, we only meant to name her after my adopted sister, who is Chinese. The name means "little sister" in Cantonese, and since she was the youngest of our three, it seemed perfect.

Later, however, my husband (who is from India where we have lived for the past ten years) remembered something. In Punjabi, his mother tongue, the word "mui" is the feminine for "dying one". Mui Mui is exactly the way many Indians pronounce Moy Moy, and Ravi's older relatives kept wondering aloud why we had chosen such an inauspicious name for our daughter.

I dismissed this as unfortunate but coincidental. It's the Cantonese meaning that matters, I insisted. After all, she's named after my Chinese sister. But recently, I learned a bit more about the Chinese word which made me realize that China and India are not all that far apart. Indeed, they are separated only by the Himalayas, where Moy Moy (coincidentally or not) is from.

What I learned concerned the Chinese name Mei-Mei, which is often given to a girl child saved from an early death. Mei-Mei, Mui-Mui. Little girls dying or saved from the grave. But Moy Moy still meant "little sister", I assured myself.

Then I read *The Joy Luck Club* by Amy Tan, a novel about Chinese-Americans in San Francisco. One of the main characters is called Mei-Mei; the name, the author explains, means "little sister". Suddenly, the whole thing became clear to me. Both in India and China, "little sister" and "girl saved from an early death" could very easily be the same thing; "little sister" and "little dying girl" even more so.

A THRIVING PRACTICE

In both countries, female infanticide is an ancient and, in many areas, still thriving practice. In China, according to Stephen Mosher, director of the Asian Studies Center at California's Claremont Institute, as late as 1980, village midwives were often instructed to "draw a bucket of water when a woman went into labor. If the new-born had the misfortune to be a girl, she was plunged into the bucket before she had a chance to draw her first breath."

Although the international demographic norm for the boy-girl ratio is 106 boys to 100 girls, in China's 1981 census, the numbers were 108.5 to 100. That translates into 232,000 missing baby girls. In 1982, the number of boys climbed to 109 and in 1983 to 111. According to the 1990 census, little has changed. *The New York Times* reported in June that perhaps five percent of all infant girls born in China are unaccounted for.

ONE-CHILD POLICY

Until 1986, China's one-child policy was strictly enforced, putting many poor parents in the hideous position of weighing their own survival against their daughter's. To the Chinese peasant, the only social security system is the rearing of a productive son. With him to support them in their old age, they can look forward to a relatively peaceful retirement. A daughter, on the other hand, must be married off at great expense, at which point her financial contributions to her parents cease. A couple who chooses to bring up a girl as their only child is either financially independent, mad, or highly principled. Most of the desperate peasants of China are none of these and many of them, apparently, kill their daughters.

Finally, in 1986, the Chinese government, due in part to international censure, relented somewhat. Couples with "real difficulties" (i.e., a girl child) could apply for permission to try again.

The second time around, then, the stakes would be obviously even higher, the chances of a second daughter surviving very slight. Just as, by the bizarre mores at work in America today, a pregnant woman is assumed to have considered her "options", to have weighed and rejected abortion, so a Chinese woman bringing up a second daughter can be assumed to have considered and rejected infanticide. The name Moy Moy or Mei Mei, with both its meanings, is frighteningly appropriate: to be a little sister means to have been saved from an early death. In India, the situation is no less grim. Although female infanticide was outlawed by the British in 1870, the practice continues. In one South Indian district, according to the news magazine *India Today* in its cover story "Born to Die" (June 1986), an estimated 6,000 baby girls had been poisoned to death in the preceding ten years.

WEALTHY WOMEN

Wealthy women have their own, more acceptable way of dealing with unwanted baby girls: amniocentesis and abortion. Although amniocentesis is now banned for sex-selection, in most cities it is

ULTRASOUND & ABORTION

Partly because of ultrasound scans to check the sex of fetuses, followed by abortion of females, the sex ratio of newborn children in China last year reached 118.5 boys for every 100 girls. That statistic, based on an official survey of 385,000 people conducted last September and October, is a preliminary one, but it so shocked the authorities that they ordered that it be kept secret.

Normally, women of all races give birth to 105 or 106 boys for every 100 girls.

Nicholas D. Kristof, "New Technology, Ancient Prejudice," **Star Tribune**, Minneapolis, July 21, 1993

still possible (often easy) to find a "doctor" willing to provide the service. In Elisabeth Bumiller's book *May You Be the Mother of a Hundred Sons: A Journey Among the Women of India*, one poor woman who had poisoned her daughter drew the obvious parallel between her action and those of wealthier women: "Abortion is costly...And you have to rest at home. So instead of spending money and losing income, we prefer to deliver the child and kill it."

The starkness of her words shocked Ms. Bumiller, who wondered whether this woman could possibly believe there was no difference between abortion and infanticide. But perhaps the realities of poverty enabled her a clearer vision than is generally afforded to the privileged elite who are so fond of subtle nuances. As another woman she interviewed put it, "Abortion at the fourth month is legally accepted in India. Instead of killing the child in the womb, I killed the child when it was born. If that is accepted, why can't I do this?"

4 GLOBAL VIOLENCE AGAINST WOMEN: AN OVERVIEW

WOMEN IN INDIA FACE ABUSE FROM BIRTH

Jim Landers

Jim Landers wrote the following article for the Dallas Morning News. *The following comments are excerpted from Landers' article.*

Points to Consider:

1. How do both tradition and technology endanger Indian females at conception?

2. Compare treatment of boys with that of girls.

3. Analyze the effect of early marriage upon females.

4. Summarize the goals of the Women's Development Project.

Jim Landers, "Many Women in India Face Abuse from Birth," **Dallas Morning News,** March, 1993. Reprinted by permission.

Tradition and technology combine today so that a woman in India is in danger from the moment she is conceived.

Bhanwari Devi learned about life as a village woman of India, wrapped in dust, cooking smoke and faded garments meant to last a lifetime. She was engaged before she was born, married at age seven and the mother of four when she was about 25... India's constitution requires equal pay for equal work by men and women. Its laws ban wife-beating and mental cruelty, child marriage and dowry, sexual enslavement, rape and sexual harassment, known as "Eve teasing".

But much of the law fails under the weight of 3,000 years of celebrating sons and despising daughters. Sons inherit. Sons bring parents wealth, a dowry worth as much as four years of a bride's family's income. A son also is essential in a Hindu family to light a parent's funeral pyre and open the way to heaven.

Daughters bring financial hardship, then leave to become servants of another family. Some female infants are killed: smothered beneath a placenta, fed poison or abandoned in the wild. More often, they simply get less than their brothers of the food and medicine needed to survive. Among children younger than five, the death rate is three times greater for girls than for boys.

FEMALE FETUSES ABORTED

Tradition and technology combine today so that a woman in India is in danger from the moment she is conceived. Hundreds of thousands of Indian parents use sex-determination tests to plan families of sons. Amniocentesis or ultrasound tests showing a female fetus are followed by abortions.

The practice began in the late 1970s. The number of abortions performed because of sex-determination tests since then is unknown. By June 1982, *The Times of India* estimated 78,000 such abortions had taken place.

The birth of a girl may bring regret, even grief, to her parents. One New Delhi mother of two girls described it as giving birth to a stone. Discrimination is such that the Indian government's 1992 action plan for girls declares "She has the right to survive" as its first premise. The plan says mothers are more likely to breastfeed sons than daughters. Boys are more likely than girls to get treatment for

25

diarrhea, which kills 1.5 million Indian children every year. Boys are much more likely to be inoculated against disease and much more likely to go to school.

The typical Indian girl lives her life in a farm village. She grows up illiterate and with two-thirds of the calories she needs to achieve her height and weight potential. One in four dies before age 15. The others marry in their teens. They have eight or nine pregnancies, six live births and raise four children before dying at an average age of 59. . .

MASS WEDDINGS ARRANGED

Devi's village is in Rajasthan, one of India's more violent states. Bhateri sits behind a range of red and chalk bluffs, its small huts spilled in the hollows. Goods come to Bhateri in carts pulled by camels, or on the backs of elephants.

Devi and Mohun Lal, her husband, have a two-acre field and a milk cow. Their oldest daughter, married when she was 14, lives in another village. Daughter Rameshawari and her two brothers still live at home. Each year, following the counsel of astrologers, villages throughout Rajasthan arrange mass weddings among brides and grooms as young as one. Devi says she does not remember her wedding to Lal. "She was seven, and I was nine," Lal says with a smile. "We were engaged even before we were born." They began living together when she was about 14.

Rajasthani village children are usually married by their 10th birthday. A girl continues to live in her father's house, at least until her first menstrual period. Then it is the father's duty to inform the boy's family that his daughter is sexually mature and ready to live with her husband.

Since 1955, India has required a girl to reach age 18 before she can marry. More than 15 percent of the girls between ages 10 and 14 are married, however. "When a girl's sent away for marriage at such a young age, she'll start having children very young as well. That means more mothers will die giving birth, and more babies will die," says Kanchan Mathur, one of the social scientists who sponsored Devi in Rajasthan's Women's Development Project.

"Some of these girls are just 10 years old. Their education comes to a halt when they're married," Mathur says. "And what do these girls know of sex? They have no idea what's happening to them."

BURNING BRIDES

He found Farhat in an undisturbed room, sitting on a stool. Ninety-seven percent of her body was covered in burns and as he carried her out of the house chunks of scorched flesh fell from her body. On her death bed, Farhat accused her husband and sister-in-law of throwing a burning oil stove at her.

In 1990 there were 1,800 deaths caused by burns from oil stoves, five per cent of the victims being females aged between 18 to 30. A more recent report claims that every six hours one Pakistani woman dies in this way.

Maria del Nevo, "The Burned Bride," **New Internationalist**, September, 1992

India marries its city girls young, too. A 12-year-old in a bad marriage in Asia's biggest slum is a nightmare almost beyond belief. And the police, the courts, the few women's shelters and even fewer human rights workers hold out just the barest hope of rescue...

WOMEN GET TRAINING

The Women's Development Project recruited Bhanwari Devi and about 1,000 other women of Rajasthan in the mid-1980s to try to improve life for village girls and women. It was a joint effort between the Rajasthan state government and a Jaipur academic center called the Institute for Development Studies.

Village women were chosen for their natural leadership. A certain independence was required as well. Many husbands opposed sending their wives to Jaipur for 2 1/2 weeks, says Kanchan Mathur, a program sponsor with the Institute.

Project workers tell other village women how to find time to attend literacy classes. They tell women how they can find contraceptives. They explain AIDS and the risks of unprotected sex. They teach women about their rights under the law and how to fight for those rights.

Devi once humiliated a schoolteacher who tried to trade grades for sex with the village children. She challenged land and water rights. She argued for equal pay among men and women employed in famine relief works.

Her achievements brought her to the attention of the chief minister of Rajasthan. The social scientists sponsoring the Women's
Development Project considered her a model for what could be
accomplished. And in 1989, the program became a national model
for combatting conditions blamed for much of the violence endured
by India's women.

What the Women's Development Project did not want to see was
the recruitment of its social workers into police work. But that is
what happened in last year's campaign against child marriages.
Rajasthan's chief minister ordered enforcement of the ban on child
marriages. He went on television ordering an end to the practice.

Devi advised Bhateri families planning to marry off their children
that they were breaking the law and risking arrest. The Gujars, a
clan representing about 40 of Bhateri's 100 families, told her to quit
interfering. She told the police about the wedding plans. The
police issued their own warnings, pasting them on the doors of the
young betrothed.

The wedding went forward at 2:00 one morning in May, two
hours later than the midnight recommendation of the local
astrologer. The family of a one-year-old girl married her to a two-
year-old boy. Men of the girl's family declared loudly that Devi
would pay a price for intruding.

VILLAGERS RETALIATE

On September 22, Devi and Lal were weeding their farm plot
about 6:00 p.m. Devi was stooped over, cutting weeds with a hand
scythe, when she heard her husband cry out. She turned and saw
five men – men she says were the little bride's uncles and cousins –
beating her husband. "Leave him alone! I am the one you want,
not my husband!" she said. Two men held Lal. The other three
wrestled Devi to the ground. While one held her down, two men
took turns raping her. They stuffed her scarf in her mouth to muffle
the screams.

It was dusk by the time the attackers fled. Devi and Lal were hurt
and dazed. She vowed to go to the police. He moaned that it was
no use, that they had no hope of justice. She insisted. The nearest
police were nine miles away, and there is no phone in Bhateri.
Devi went to two families in the village seeking help. Both turned
her away.

At daybreak, Devi and her husband took a bus to the home of

28

another woman who worked with the Women's Development Project. She took them to another village, Bassi, where there was a police station. A deputy police superintendent listened to her story with skepticism. Asked why he was so hostile, he responded, "Madam, do you know the meaning of rape?"

The doctor at the Bassi clinic refused to examine her for evidence of rape. So her friends in the Women's Development Project took her to a hospital in Jaipur with instructions from the Bassi clinic. When they handed over the instructions, however, the hospital staff said they asked only that Devi be examined to confirm her age. A rape examination would require an order from a magistrate. The magistrate told Devi, Lal and the Women's Project workers to come to court the next morning.

Forty-eight hours after she was raped, Devi finally underwent a medical examination. She had not bathed since the attack, but the results that came back were of no use to the police. Women's Development Project staffers say the amount of time that passed and the cursory nature of the exam rendered it useless.

Devi and Lal were sent back to the Bassi police station. The police told Devi to leave her dress with them as evidence. She had no other clothes. She wrapped herself in her husband's bloodstained turban and, at 1:00 a.m., walked two miles to the home of a friend.

The police came to Bhateri three days after Devi and her husband were attacked. Villagers said the accused Gujars were away at another village buying mustard seeds at the time of the assault. Six months later, the police had made no arrests.

Prime Minister P.V. Narasimha Rao ordered the Central Bureau of Investigation, India's equivalent of the FBI, to take charge of the case. He offered 10,000 rupees of his own money to compensate Devi for her suffering. Devi says she suffered a mental breakdown in December and still battles depression. Lal is asked how he feels about the gang rape of his wife. He says nothing for a moment. Devi answers for him: "If it had not happened before his eyes, he would have said I was corrupted, that I had done wrong, and he would have turned me away from my home. Isn't that right?"

Lal is silent for a moment. Then, quietly and evenly, he says: "Yes. I saw it. I know she's telling the truth."

5   GLOBAL VIOLENCE AGAINST WOMEN: AN OVERVIEW

SEXUAL SLAVERY IN THAILAND

Gayle Reaves

Gayle Reaves wrote the following article for the Dallas Morning News. *The following comments are excerpts from Reaves' article.*

Points to Consider:

1. Describe how Thai girls are being turned into commerce.

2. Tell how government efforts to stem prostitution are hampered.

3. How is the AIDS epidemic tied to Thai prostitution?

4. What are the international ramifications of the Thai sex industry?

Gayle Reaves, **Dallas Morning News**, March, 1993. Reprinted by permission.

Girls from the Akha tribe in northern Thailand wear traditional village clothing. Daughters of poor tribal families are often sold by their parents to agents of the sex trade.

At an age when many American teens are trying to talk Dad out of the car keys, she sits on the floor of a shabby cottage, trying to talk her frail, gaunt father out of sending her back to a brothel. At 17, she already has worked in three brothels, because of the need to help support her ailing parents.

In the dim interior of the cottage – bought with her prostitution wages – her father argues with social workers who want her to live and study at their shelter. She is their only child, the father says. The brothel agent owns the land on which the house sits, and that day he has threatened to evict them. The father has borrowed more money from the agent, with his daughter's work as collateral. What will happen to them if they lose her wages?

He does not understand that, soon enough, he may lose her anyway. She has the AIDS virus. An hour's drive north of Mae Chan, teacher Jandraem Sirikhampoo calls a group of students to her side. These little girls, she says, were sold as babies by their parents. The buyers are raising them, like livestock, to be sold into prostitution. Most buyers, she says, already have sold their own daughters.

"It happens quite often," says Jandraem, who founded the school for poor children. "The kids know...that they have to go to Bangkok at a certain age." She is searching for foster families for them, ignoring threats from brothel agents.

These girls and thousands like them are the clouded future of Thailand. A generation of girls are being turned into commerce: they are traded by their families or kidnappers for houses, water buffalo, land, cash, food – and televisions. Many girls now accept prostitution as their fate, the only way to support families whose rural ways of life are disappearing.

Thailand has become the red-light district to much of the world. In a country of 56 million people, relief agencies estimate there are two million prostitutes; as many as 800,000 of them are children. Perhaps one in 12 women and older children may be involved, and up to 80 percent of the girls in some tribal villages.

Prostitution in Thailand often amounts to slavery: children cannot give consent, and many others are held in captivity or debt bondage. It can be a fatal servitude. Thailand is the center of what experts say soon will soon be the worst AIDS epidemic in the world.

Slavery has been internationally condemned since long before the United Nations set out its human rights manifesto in 1948. But in Thailand, sexual slavery, for the most part, has been internationally ignored.

SEX INDUSTRY

In the past few years, international and Thai women's groups and children's rights groups – plus the fear of AIDS – have led the Thai government to step up raids against sex businesses involving child prostitutes. A bill in the Thai Parliament proposes to increase penalties for pimps and procurers.

But such efforts are hampered by the economic and political strength of the sex industry. Government officials acknowledge that police corruption is a major problem. The huge Thai sex industry originally developed to serve U.S. air bases and soldiers on leave from the Vietnam War. It is now a drawing card for male tourists and workers from Japan, Malaysia, Burma, the Middle East, Europe and the United States.

Nor is the problem confined to Thailand: prostitution and sexual slavery are on the rise again in China, and Thai prostitutes are exported to Japan and Germany. AIDS researchers say "sex tourism" is a growing problem in the Philippines, Brazil, the Dominican Republic, Kenya and Eastern Europe.

Tourism has become Thailand's leading industry. The government discourages the marketing of Thailand for sex tourism, but the crowds at the live-sex shows in Bangkok's Patpong district still seem to rival those at the Buddhist temples.

Sexual services for a price are available all over Bangkok, from the poorest slums to the prime minister's neighborhood. In the city of 10 million people, separate streets cater to Japanese businessmen, Chinese and Westerners.

Muslim men flock to southern Thailand for paid sex, which they cannot obtain in their own countries. In some southern Thai cities, says child-rights worker Sanphasit Koompraphant, "every day you can see buses coming from Singapore – and their passengers are 100 percent men. In every block, there is a hotel, 20 stories. There is no tourist business there, no industry – only lumber plantations and sex services."

But foreign trade represents only a small part of Thailand's prosti-tution business. Relief workers say 80 percent of the customers are Thai men. AIDS researcher Vicharn Vithayasai says that going to a brothel is as common and acceptable among Thai men as having a beer after work.

The sex industry has outstripped the supply of available Thai women. Gangs now operate in Burma, Laos, Vietnam and China, luring or kidnapping thousands of girls each year. They are put to work in upper-class "teahouses", garish bars and hidden brothels. Or they end up in one of the thousands of other businesses — mas-sage parlors, go-go clubs, coffee shops, hotels and shacks — from which sex is dispensed in Thailand. More than 40,000 girls and women are believed to have been lured or kidnapped from Burma alone.

It is not only women's bodies that are being sold — it is their lives. Relief agencies estimate more than 40 percent of Thai prosti-tutes test positive for the AIDS virus. Thailand is the nucleus of an expected AIDS pandemic poised to rip a deadly path through the future of southern Asia. Relief workers fear that entire hill tribes in northern Thailand and Burma will be wiped out.

Prostitutes already are dying from AIDS, but little notice is taken, says Sanphasit, child-rights director for the Bangkok-based Foundation for Children. Thai society "cares much more about the health of the clients...(than) about the women who work in broth-els," he says...

33

POLICE CORRUPTION

Police corruption in Thailand is one of the main stumbling blocks in the government's attempts to attack sexual slavery. Relief workers say that police not only are paid to ignore and protect the brothels but also are often part owners.

Police corruption "is the toughest question" in the prostitution equation, says Tawat Wichaidit, secretary-general to Prime Minister Chuan Leekpai. Tawat says that corrupt and honest elements within Thai police departments "are fighting each other" and that the government has pledged to do everything it can to change the system. He is setting up his own team to investigate prostitution-related corruption...

Relief workers are skeptical of the government's commitment – and resources – to fight an industry that brings so much wealth. But they welcome the new willingness to discuss it as a serious problem.

At the New Life Center, Dau sews and studies. Happy with her life there, she doesn't think much about what lies ahead. Because of the pressures on her family, she cannot go home permanently.

Dau has the AIDS virus but doesn't understand its implications. For now, her plans are only to stay at New Life and to make the hat covered with needlework, coins and other trinkets that will complete her traditional Akha outfit.

6   GLOBAL VIOLENCE AGAINST WOMEN: AN OVERVIEW

CHILDBIRTH AND DEATH IN POOR NATIONS

Jodi L. Jacobson

Jodi L. Jacobson is a senior researcher at the Worldwatch Institute. She covers women's health and population issues. Worldwatch *is a bimonthly magazine published by the Worldwatch Institute in Washington, D.C.*

Points to Consider:

1. Contrast maternal mortality in developing countries with that of North America and Northern Europe.

2. Explain the medical factors that contribute to maternal mortality.

3. What economic and political factors enter into maternal mortality?

4. What is the focus of the International Safe Motherhood Initiative?

Jodi L. Jacobson, "Making the World Safe for Democracy," **Worldwatch**, February, 1991. Reprinted by permission.

In fact, complications of pregnancy and illegal abortion are the leading killers of Third World women in their twenties and thirties.

Women of the Bariba ethnic group in Benin have long been taught to view having babies as a test of will. To endure labor and childbirth alone, in silence, and without complaint, is a sure path to social esteem. To request help is to admit weakness and invite shame. As a result, many women die needlessly when complications arise.

The ensuing high rates of maternal morbidity and mortality – illnesses and deaths from problems related to pregnancy and childbirth – are the common threads that tie Bariba women to their sisters in societies throughout the Third World.

THE MIDDLE AGES

In relative terms, most women in developing countries are still bearing children as if it were the Middle Ages. One in 21 pregnant women in Africa, one in 38 in South Asia, and one in 73 in South America will die from complications of pregnancy and childbirth this year. By contrast, only one in every 7,000 in North America and one in 10,000 in Northern Europe will suffer a similar fate.

The World Health Organization (WHO) estimates, on the basis of incomplete official statistics, that some 500,000 women die annually from maternal complications. Privately, many experts believe better data collection might show the figure to be at least twice that.

In fact, complications of pregnancy and illegal abortion are the leading killers of Third World women in their twenties and thirties. What is more, for every woman who dies, 15 to 20 others suffer serious health problems that affect their ability to provide for themselves and their families.

MEDICAL CAUSES

To the established list of medical causes of maternal mortality, which includes hemorrhage, obstructed labor, and toxemia (a condition of high blood pressure that can lead to convulsions), must now be added new and growing threats like the mounting reliance on unsafe abortion, an increase in teenage pregnancies, and the spread of AIDS. Illness and death will claim a growing share of women in their prime unless action is taken to lessen the dangers of pregnancy and childbirth.

The social and economic toll of these losses is incalculable. Working up to 18 hours a day to gather fuelwood, fetch water, market surplus goods in rural areas, or earn income as street vendors or day-laborers in cities, women are often the sole source of nurture and economic support for their families. A maternal death therefore represents far more than the loss of a single productive member of society.

Studies show that the death of a mother often leaves her children at greater risk of malnutrition, abuse, neglect, exploitation, and premature death. Hence, a sizable proportion of the nearly 15 million deaths among Third World children under the age of five each year may be traced to the pregnancy-related death or disabling of their mothers.

As much a social, economic, and political problem as a medical one, the plight of mothers throughout the Third World bears singular testimony to the powerlessness of women in these societies. Discriminated against from infancy, a female child often receives insufficient food and health care, and is given less education than a boy.

As a married woman, she is more often than not denied by law or social custom the right to own or inherit property, to obtain credit, or to control her fertility without the consent of male relatives. Her surest route to status and security is to bear many children, preferably sons. But chronic malnutrition, poor health, and illiteracy make childbearing risky.

WOMEN'S HEALTH

Historically, women's health has ranked low on the totem pole of international priorities. But in 1987, WHO joined with the United

Nations Population Fund and the World Bank at a conference in Nairobi, Kenya, to hammer out the International Safe Motherhood Initiative, a plan of action directed at improving maternal health. Since that time, a number of regional conferences have been held to identify specific problems and priorities...

Assisting women to practice birth spacing, reduce the overall number of pregnancies, and reduce the proportion that fall under the age of 19 and over 36 – a major focus of the initiative – would prevent as many as half of all maternal deaths.

Moreover, family planning could be instrumental in reducing reliance on unsafe abortion – which alone is responsible for the deaths of at least 200,000 women each year – as well as reducing transmission of the HIV virus. AIDS has dire implications for maternal health, particularly in Africa. A survey by the United Nations Children's Fund estimates that more than three million women in Africa will die of AIDS in the 1990s, leaving more than five million AIDS orphans.

STRATEGY AND CHANGES

No strategy can ultimately achieve success unless women become equal partners in development. A call for systematic changes in the nature of policies and the allocation of resources toward women are an integral part of the Safe Motherhood Initiative. Such changes run the gamut from the social to the technological, including efforts to increase female education, the enforcement of legislation improving women's status, and the development of labor-saving technologies.

The obstacles to improving maternal health will be insurmountable, however, without a massive effort by the international community, paralled by national governments and women's groups, to change the attitudes, laws, and practices that discriminate against women. But, with few exceptions, the goals to which many countries have ascribed in rhetorical terms have yet to be acted upon.

Meanwhile, for Third World women, it will not be safe to be pregnant as long as it remains unsafe to be female.

7 GLOBAL VIOLENCE AGAINST WOMEN: AN OVERVIEW

WOMEN BEAR THE BRUNT OF POVERTY

Oxfam America

The following article is excerpted from literature published by Oxfam America, an organization devoted to the fight against poverty and hunger. Oxfam America is located at 26 West Street, Boston, Massachusetts 02111-1206.

Points to Consider:

1. List some laws and traditions that create poverty among women.

2. Contrast the effect of "development" upon women with the effect upon men.

3. Summarize Oxfam's program to help impoverished women.

Excerpted from a public statement by Oxfam America titled "Simply Put, Women Bear the Brunt of Poverty," 1993. Reprinted by permission.

Seventy to 80 percent of the world's refugees are women and children.

Women, in most societies, bear a double burden – raising children and providing food for their families. Yet, in many of those same societies, women have few rights. Laws and traditions perpetuate sexual discrimination – and the poverty it helps create – by preventing women from owning land, getting credit, or protecting themselves in the home and workplace.

This backwardness contributes to a plethora of problems: abortion and infanticide of girls, domestic violence, the abuse of domestic help, the destruction of families, and the rampant spread of AIDS among women, to name just a few. Women aren't the only victims of discrimination – children, men, families, and communities all suffer. Women grow half of the world's food, but own only one percent of the world's land.

Women head 20 to 30 percent of all households in the global South, and 50 percent in some Latin American cities, many rural areas of Africa, and regions suffering from war. Yet in many countries, women cannot own land, open a bank account, get commercial credit, or sign a contract.

Domestic violence is epidemic and under-reported throughout the world. Women frequently don't take part in development programs, or drop out of them, because of pressure from their husbands. Seventy to 80 percent of the world's refugees are women and children, yet relief efforts often don't take into account their particular

18-HOUR DAYS

Every time I return home to my native Bangladesh, I come face-to-face with the devastating burden that hunger, poverty, and discrimination bring to the lives of poor women.

If you could travel with me, you would see it for yourself.

You would encounter women who are denied basic rights – the opportunity to attend school, learn to read, receive health care, earn a decent living, or own land.

You'd meet women who routinely work 18 hour days – rising each morning before dawn, spending two to three hours collecting firewood and hauling water, putting in a day of back-breaking work in the rice fields, and returning home to prepare dinner, tend to children, and clean house.

You would hear the stories of women denied bank credit because of their gender, women forced to turn to money lenders charging 150% interest and risking violence and abuse in the event of late payment.

And, you would meet widows, divorced and disabled women who not only endure lives of poverty and suffer from poor health, but also are often excluded from participation in community life.

Such hardships and barriers to opportunity for women are not unique to my homeland. Poor and landless women share a common plight in many of the impoverished nations in which Oxfam America works.

Fanzia E. Ahmed, **Oxfam America**, July 1993

health, nutritional, and economic needs.

In some Asian countries the preference for boys has resulted in female infanticide and death by neglect on a massive scale – creating millions of "missing" women. If women were paid for their domestic labor, they would add $4 trillion to the global economy – one-third of the world's annual economic product. Women are the key to healthy, productive families and communities.

Oxfam America helps women become more economically secure,

WOMEN & DEVELOPMENT

Until recently, women in all traditional societies combined diverse economic activities with their child-care responsibilities and domestic tasks. But the process called "development" frequently removes women like Dona Maria from their economic roles while simultaneously excluding them from a "modern" economy. All too often, a growing reliance on cash crops, wage labor, and commercial craft production – that is, the usual indicators of development – obscure, even eliminate, women as economic actors. It is the men of a community who seem to gain access to new technology, training, jobs, and credit and other resources.

Frances Abrahamer Rothstein, "Women's Work, Women's Worth,"
Cultural Survival Quarterly, Winter 1992

and increase their independence and decision making power in the home and community. Around the world, Oxfam America supports literacy and numeracy courses, technical and leadership training, credit programs, and small business loans. These projects include child-care provisions and other assistance, so women can increase their productivity, rather than increasing their already heavy work loads. And many projects bring women and men together to find more equal ways of sharing hardships and rewards.

Oxfam America works with local groups and community organizations that respond to the needs of the people they serve. We identify local groups with women in leadership roles, and ask all our partners to incorporate women into every phase of their operations. We encourage women to organize, because again and again we have seen the strength women derive from working together.

8   GLOBAL VIOLENCE AGAINST WOMEN: AN OVERVIEW

WOMEN AND VIOLENCE IN NATIVE CULTURES

Cultural Survival Quarterly

The following statement is excerpted form an article that appeared in Cultural Survival Quarterly, *a journal dealing with indigenous people and their problems of survival around the world.*

Points to Consider:

1. Summarize the role of indigenous women.

2. How does contact with larger political systems hurt women?

3. Contrast the contributions by women with their treatment by the world.

"Women and Identity," **Cultural Survival Quarterly**, Fall, 1991. Reprinted by permission.

Modernization and the changeover to market economies have mobilized some indigenous women and left others stranded.

Throughout the 1970s and 1980s, issues relating to women and helping the poorest of the poor dominated development agencies, not to mention the lip service many agencies – large and small, public and private – gave to program priorities. Surely, indigenous women are the poorest of the poor, among the planet's least represented and the most exploited.

Women's position in indigenous societies has not always been ideal; there is no reason to attempt to paint it so. Contact by and integration into larger economic and political systems could actually improve some women's status, but this is not usually the case. When indigenous societies join larger systems, this leads to a further masculinization of politics, and integrating these groups into other legal traditions often erodes women's traditional rights to land and resources. Furthermore, women in partially assimilated societies rarely control funds – even those generated by their own efforts.

Most seriously, perhaps, the women and children they attempt to protect are most often the first victims of armed conflict between indigenous nations and political states – the majority of the 5 million people killed, the 15 million who flee their countries as refugees, and the 150 million who have been displaced from their homelands. The burdens of survival – how to feed their families and reassemble their lives in new, unfamiliar settings – rest on them.

Indigenous women are the protectors of language. They teach their children their own language and are the last to learn the language of the outsiders. Through language they keep alive world views as well as extensive knowledge of their people's resources. And women are the seed savers. Most often they are the ones who plant, gather, and cultivate the vast majority of their community's food. In increasing numbers, too, indigenous women are organizing to fight the harmful effects that contact and integration with the outside world have on their families and their cultures.

Indigenous peoples were not poor prior to Western contact; only by being integrated into systems that put them at the bottom of the ladder have they become impoverished. Likewise, indigenous women have not been marginalized in their traditional societies; this only happens when they become integrated into Western-dominated societies. It is no accident that indigenous women receive

44

WOMEN, POVERTY AND VIOLENCE

Women make up more than half the population of the planet. We provide 66% of industrial work hours and 75% of the agricultural labor of the world. Yet women earn one-tenth of the world's income and own less than one-hundredth of the world's property. Violence against women is epidemic, the most common form of human rights abuse on earth. Eighty percent of the refugees from war are women and children. In the U.S., 84% of those living in poverty are women and children.

"Women vs. Violence," **Peace and Freedom**, January/February, 1991

wages that are about 60 percent of those earned by their male counterparts. With contact comes the widespread replication of these Western values throughout the world.

9 GLOBAL VIOLENCE AGAINST WOMEN: AN OVERVIEW

STDs: THE OTHER EPIDEMIC

Jodi L. Jacobson

Jodi L. Jacobson is a senior researcher at the Worldwatch Institute. She covers women's health and population issues. Worldwatch *is a bimonthly magazine published by the Worldwatch Institute in Washington, D.C.*

Points to Consider:

1. Contrast the toll of STDs on women as compared to men.

2. List some of the most common STDs.

3. Briefly describe methods to prevent and cure STDs.

4. Analyze factors leading to the STD epidemic among women.

Sexually transmitted diseases are running rampant, taking a greater toll on women's lives than does AIDS in men, women, and children combined. The cure for these infections is cheap – simple contraceptive prevention – but neglected.

In the tradition of the Haya tribe of northwestern Tanzania, a husband may divorce his wife if she proves to be infertile, effectively leaving her destitute. In other parts of Africa and Asia, infertile women routinely are subject to abandonment, abuse, and even murder. The irony is that although women bear the blame for it, around 70 percent of female infertility in developing countries is caused by sexually transmitted diseases that can be traced back to their husbands or partners.

In Africa, infertility is epidemic among poor rural females whose husbands migrate to urban areas in search of work and return home with more than a paycheck to share. The vast majority of Africa's migrant workers live in cities where both the demand for prostitutes and the level of sexually transmitted diseases are high. Women, especially female prostitutes, are often blamed for the spread of these infections. Studies by the World Bank and others confirm, though, that it is men seeking commercial sex who carry infection from one prostitute to another – and eventually even to their wives and girlfriends.

In a vicious cycle, these patterns of behavior reinforce the subordinate position of women in society. Men become infected through visits to prostitutes, who "choose" their profession from sheer lack of economic alternatives. Men transmit diseases to their wives, who are powerless either to prevent or treat them. Infection leads to infertility, which leads to divorce. In some cases, the ex-wife herself turns to prostitution to survive.

Yet infertility is just one of several conditions caused in women by a group of sexually transmitted diseases (STDs) that includes chanchroid, chlamydia, gonorrhea, herpes, human papillomavirus, and syphilis. Cervical cancer, inflammation of the uterus, and ectopic pregnancy are some of the other life-threatening conditions that stem from these diseases.

These STDs take a disproportionate toll on women's lives. They cause far more death and illness in women than does AIDS – another STD – in men, women, and children combined. They also cause a large share of preventable infant deaths and disability each year. They reduce individual economic productivity, hamper efforts to slow population growth, and burden already poor health care systems. And worse yet, most STDs actually facilitate transmission of the AIDS virus.

All these infections can be prevented or treated; unlike AIDS, most can be cured. Through better family planning programs, increased accessibility of STD testing and treatment, and, most important, improvements in the status of women, the spread of such infections could be curtailed sharply. For want of such initiatives, these "other" STDs continue to spread unchecked and relatively unnoticed throughout the world.

PROFILE OF A KILLER

All told, infection rates of most STDs appear to be the same in males and females. "But women and infants," warn A. de Schryver and Andre Meheus of the World Health Organization (WHO), "bear the major burden of complications and serious [consequences]." Typically, infections in men cause mild to severe genital or urinary tract problems; in rare cases, they cause sterility and death.

For women, it's a different story. Currently, STDs and "reproductive tract infections", a broader grouping to which STDs belong, cause at least 750,000 deaths and 75 million illnesses among women each year worldwide. Indications are that the number of these deaths will more than double by 2000. Death rates are rising fastest in Africa, followed by Asia, and then Latin America.

Cervical cancer caused by the sexually transmitted human papillomavirus alone accounts for nearly half of these losses. About 450,000 cases of potentially fatal reproductive tract cancers are diagnosed annually. Of these, an estimated 354,000 occur in Third World women, virtually all of whom die due to lack of access to relatively simple early treatment measures. In fact, in developing countries where the viruses that cause them are spreading like wildfire, deaths from cervical cancers already outrank those from all other cancers in women combined. Complications of other infections also are running rampant.

Worldwide, about 250 million new infections – including chlamydia, gonorrhea, and the human papillomavirus – are sexually transmitted each year [see Table 1 on next page]. These STDs outrank AIDS in both the numbers of people infected and the annual

48

increase in new cases. Chlamydia and the human papillomavirus, for example, account for 50 million and 30 million new cases per year, respectively. HIV, the AIDS virus, infected one million people worldwide between April and December 1991, according to the WHO.

AN EPIDEMIC

According to de Schryver and Meheus, STDs and other reproductive tract infections are epidemic in many developing countries. In fact, a study in the Indian state of Maharashtra revealed that 92 percent of the 650 rural women examined had one or more gynecological or sexual disease, with an astonishing average of 3.6 such infections per woman. Less than eight percent of the women in the survey had ever undergone a gynecological examination in the past. "Obviously," concluded study author Rani Bang and colleagues at SEARCH, a nongovernmental health organization in Maharashtra, "there is a large gap between the need and the care."

Spot surveys in other countries have produced similarly alarming results. For instance, a study in two rural Egyptian villages found that half of 509 non-pregnant women aged 20 to 60 years had infections. Twenty-two percent of 3,000 women canvassed in Bangladesh reported symptoms of reproductive tract infections. The actual number of those infected but not reporting symptoms was believed to be twice as high.

Table 1. Number of New Sexually Transmitted Infections Worldwide, 1990

Infection	Number of New Infections (millions)
Trichomoniasis	120
Chlamydia	50
Human Papillomavirus	30
Gonorrhea	25
Herpes	20
Syphilis	4
Chancroid	2
Human Immunodeficiency Virus (HIV)	1

Source: World Health Organization

THE GENDER FACTOR

Behavioral patterns are key to the spread of STDs. Some of these are perpetuated by dangerous myths regarding health practices. Throughout sub-Saharan Africa, for example, traditional healers promote the idea that men infected with STDs should have sex with virgins to cure themselves, a belief contributing to the uncontrolled spread of these diseases now evident among adolescent girls in that region.

Others are the product of social expectation. In many countries, assessments of sexual behavior show that men tend to have a larger number of sexual partners than women. High rates of premarital sex often result from the belief that males should be sexually experienced from an early age, and females chaste until marriage. In Guatemala and Ecuador, for example, the transition to "manhood" supposedly requires a young male to have his first intercourse with a prostitute...

A QUESTION OF STATUS

While far more women find themselves at risk because of their partners' behavior rather than their own, they are even less likely than their partners to be able to protect themselves from infection. The use of condoms would markedly reduce the risk of infection, yet in many societies the prerogative of choosing what birth control method to use, and whether to use one at all, lies with the man.

WHAT CAN BE DONE

It is at once heartening and frustrating to realize that strategies to prevent and cure STDs – many of which are the same, not only to combat AIDS but to improve maternal and infant health – are inexpensive.

That a combination of coordinated strategies and a relatively small allocation of resources by governments could make tremendous public gains in several areas is more than encouraging. The frustration arises from the fact that few governments and health agencies throughout the world recognize these diseases as a priority...

These initiatives alone, promising as they may be, cannot be counted on to win the battle against sexually transmitted diseases. Unless governments and international health organizations muster their resources to wage an all-out war on STDs – including prevention, testing, and cure – the number of women dying from such infections will continue to multiply.

10 GLOBAL VIOLENCE AGAINST WOMEN: AN OVERVIEW

MASSIVE VIOLENCE IN AMERICA

The Unforgettable Fire

The following article originally appeared in The Unforgettable Fire, *a magazine which explores women's spirituality through articles, poetry and fiction.* The Unforgettable Fire *is located at P.O. Box 388, Lyndhurst, New Jersey 07071.*

Points to Consider:

1. Provide several examples of domestic violence in the United States.

2. What do the statistics imply?

3. Who are the homeless?

"So Women Are Better Off Today?" **The Unforgettable Fire**, July, 1992. Reprinted by permission.

So Women Are Better Off Today?

- A woman is beaten every twelve seconds in the United States by her spouse or significant other.

- Violent crimes against women account for more injuries and deaths to women than auto accidents, rapes, muggings, and household accidents combined.

- One third of women in the United States are currently victims of domestic violence.

- Seventy-four percent of all murders of women from domestic violence occur after the woman has left the relationship, filed for divorce, received a divorce, or filed an order of protection against the abuser. When women leave abusive relationships, the violence against them escalates.

- One hundred percent of the prisoners at Illinois' women's penal farm reported incest or sexual abuse as children. Seventy to ninety percent of all prisoners (men and women) in the United States experienced incest or sexual abuse as children.

- The rate of violent crimes against women aged twenty to twenty-four has escalated by fifty percent in this decade, while violent crimes against men in the same age range have decreased by

Cartoon by Richard Wright. Reprinted with permission.

twelve percent.

- Murder is the second leading cause of death among young women in the United States and the leading cause of death in the workplace.

- The United States has a rate of crimes against women that is higher than any other country:
  twenty times higher than Japan
  thirteen times higher than Great Britain
  four times higher than the former West Germany

- Four women a day are murdered as a result of domestic disputes.

- Thirty percent of women murdered in America are killed by their husbands or boyfriends.

- Three to four million women in the United States are beaten by their partners each year. As many as 15 million women have been abused at some time during their lives.

- In the 1980s, almost half of all homeless women were refugees of domestic violence.

- As of 1988, one-third of the one million battered women who sought emergency shelter could find none.

- In the United States, there are three times as many animal shelters as there are shelters for victims of domestic violence.

11 GLOBAL VIOLENCE AGAINST WOMEN: AN OVERVIEW

RAPE IN AMERICA

The National Women's Study

The National Women's Study is a survey of a large national sample of adult American women. Results of the study have appeared in Rape in America: A Report to the Nation, *a publication of the National Victim Center.*

Points to Consider:

1. How prevalent is rape in America?

2. Explain the discrepancy in number of rapes reported by the National Women's Study with reports from the National Crime Survey (NCS).

3. Why is rape in America a tragedy of youth?

"Rape in America: A Report to the Nation," **National Victim Center**, April 23, 1992. Reprinted by permission.

"...rape in America is a tragedy of youth..."

The past year has witnessed unprecedented interest in crimes against women, from Congressional hearings to several high profile rape trials to media scrutiny of rape issues. This intense public concern has produced more questions than answers about crimes against women...

Rape in America: A Report to the Nation addresses these and other pertinent questions, providing the first national empirical data about forcible rape of women in America...

The National Women's Study is a survey of a large national sample of 4,008 adult American women (age 18 or older), 2,008 of whom represent a cross section of all adult women and 2,000 of whom are an oversample of younger women between the ages of 18 and 34. Eighty-five percent of women contacted agreed to participate and completed the initial (Wave One) telephone interview. At the one year follow-up (Wave Two), 81% of *The National Women's Study* participants were located and re-interviewed. The two year follow-up (Wave Three) is currently in progress...

FORCIBLE RAPE

During Wave One of the study, information was gathered about forcible rape experiences occurring any time during a woman's lifetime. Thirteen percent of women surveyed reported having been victims of at least one completed rape in their lifetimes. Based on U.S. Census estimates of the number of adult women in America, one out of every eight adult women, or at least 12.1 million American women, have been the victim of forcible rape sometime in their lifetime.

Many American women were raped more than once. While 56%, or an estimated 6.8 million women experienced only one rape, 39%, or an estimated 4.7 million women were raped more than once, and five percent were unsure as to the number of times they were raped.

Prior to this study, national information about rape was limited to data on reported rapes from the FBI Uniform Crime Reports or data from the Bureau of Justice Statistics, National Crime Survey (NCS) on reported and non-reported rapes occurring in the past year. However, the NCS provides no information about rapes occurring over the lifetime of a victim, and has been recently redesigned due to criticisms that it failed to detect a substantial proportion of rape

Cartoon by Richard Wright. Reprinted with permission.

cases. Therefore, the results of these two new surveys fill a large gap in current knowledge about rape at the national level.

THE NATIONAL WOMEN'S STUDY

Information from the National Women's Study indicates that 0.7% of all women surveyed had experienced a completed forcible rape in the past year. This equates to an estimated 683,000 adult American women who were raped during a twelve-month period.

The National Women's Study estimate that 683,000 adult American women were raped in a one-year period does not include all rapes that occurred in America that year. Rapes that occurred to female children and adolescents under the age of 18 – which comprised more than six out of ten of all rapes occurring over women's lifetimes – were not included, nor were any rapes of boys or men.

Thus, the 683,000 rapes of adult women probably constitute well less than half of all the rapes that were experienced by all Americans of all ages and genders during that one-year period.

COMPARING STUDIES

How do these estimates from The National Women's Study compare with those from the FBI Uniform Crime Reports and from the

National Crime Survey? The FBI estimate of the number of attempted or completed forcible rapes that were reported to police in 1990 was 102,560. The National Crime Survey estimates include both reported and non-reported rapes that are either attempted or completed. The NCS estimate for 1990 is 130,000 attempted or completed rapes of female Americans age 12 or older. The National Women's Study estimate was based on completed rapes of adult women (age 18 or older) that occurred between Wave One (conducted in the fall of of 1989), and Wave Two (conducted in the fall of 1990). Thus, the time periods were not identical, but were roughly comparable for these three estimates. Although it did not include attempted rapes or rapes of adolescents between the ages of 12 and 18 as did the NCS, The National Women's Study estimate was still 5.3 times larger than the NCS estimate.

THREE RAPES PER PERSON

In The National Women's Study, information was gathered regarding up to three rapes per person: the first rape she ever experienced, the most recent rape, and the "worst" rape if other than the first or most recent. Information was available from Wave One about 714 such cases of rape that 507 victims of rape had experienced. The survey found that rape in America is a tragedy of youth, with the majority of rape cases occurring during childhood and adolescence. Twenty-nine percent of all forcible rapes occurred when the victim was less than 11 years old, while another 32% occurred between the ages of 11 and 17. Slightly more than five rapes (22%) occurred between the ages of 18 and 24; seven percent occurred between the ages of 25 and 29, with only six percent occurring when the victim was older than 29 years old. Three percent of the respondents were not sure or refused to answer.

12 GLOBAL VIOLENCE AGAINST WOMEN: AN OVERVIEW

BATTERED WOMEN

Dale H. Robinson

Dale H. Robinson is an analyst in Social Legislation in the Education and Public Welfare Division of the Congressional Research Service (CRS), Library of Congress.

Points to Consider:

1. Define spouse abuse.

2. Restate Dr. Lenore Walker's definition of the "battered woman syndrome".

3. How might discrepancies between the NCS and UCR and the Straus and Gelles survey be explained?

4. Compare / contrast wife to husband violence with husband to wife violence.

Dale H. Robinson, "Family Violence," Congressional Research Service, The Library of Congress, April 10, 1992.

*...the term "battered woman syndrome" was coined by
Dr. Lenore Walker to refer to characteristics common
among abused women.*

BACKGROUND

There is no one definition of spouse abuse, and estimates of the
level of spouse abuse vary depending on how the term is defined.
While there is general agreement among researchers that extreme
cases of violence, where a spouse is seriously injured or killed, constitutes spouse abuse, there is absence of consensus among
researchers as to the severity of violence that is considered to be
"abuse". Spouse abuse may include overt physical abuse, sexual
violence, or psychological abuse which may include economic
domination, intimidation, threats, and isolation. Physical and sexual abuse have received the most attention from researchers and the
media...

The nuances of spouse abuse are different from child abuse: most
victims are women; and neighbors and relatives are less apt to
report such abuse often because the victim is an adult and many
believe she should be able to handle the situation (versus children
who cannot). However, in 1979, the term "battered woman syndrome" was coined by Dr. Lenore Walker to refer to a series of characteristics common among abused women. This syndrome helped
to explain why victims remained in relationships with their abusers
and why victims of spouse abuse should be seen as people in need
of help. Some of the characteristics of this syndrome are: the perception of loss of control; the development of skills such as indirect
expression of anger and denial in order to cope with the violence
occurring; and the development of certain behaviors such as anxi-
ety, fear, confused thinking, lack of trust, and guilt...

INCIDENCE AND CHARACTERISTICS

No one organization collects national data on reported incidents
of spouse abuse. Although it is believed that this crime is severely
under-reported, estimates on the extent of spouse abuse are based
on only a handful of studies...

This section briefly presents and discusses estimates from two
major studies, by Straus and Gelles, conducted 10 years apart, that
used a national sample. Data from the National Crime Survey, conducted by the Department of Justice and the FBI Uniform Crime
Reports are also presented.

Cartoon by Carol & Simpson. Reprinted with permission.

STRAUS AND GELLES

In 1975, Straus and Gelles conducted a national survey using a representative random sample. Published in 1980 under the title *Behind Closed Doors: Violence in the American Family*, it measured reported violence among 2,100 couples. In 1985, Straus and Gelles repeated the survey with 3,500 couples. Both surveys measured reported violence by husbands toward their wives as well as by wives toward husbands, but did not include divorced or separated couples. It is important to read any differences between the 1975 and 1985 results with caution due to differences in methodology and other factors.

Overall violence included the following acts: throwing something at a spouse; pushing; biting or hitting with fist; hitting or attempting to hit with an object; "beating up"; threatening or using a knife or a gun. Severe violence was defined as those acts that have a relatively high probability of causing an injury and included acts ranging from kicking to using a knife or a gun.

Straus and Gelles reported the following rates of violence in their 1985 survey:

• the overall rate for husband to wife violence was measured at

113 per 1000 couples, representing over six million wives beaten.

* the severe violence rate for husband to wife violence was measured as 30 per 1000 couples, representing 1.6 million wives severely beaten.

In discussing their findings, Straus and Gelles state that the rate of wife to husband violence is similar to the above rates. However, because of their greater average size, strength, and aggressiveness, men are much more likely to injure their wives than wives are to injure their husbands with a given act of violence. And more importantly, the reasons why wives are violent against their husbands are often ones of retaliation or self-defense.

THE NATIONAL CRIME SURVEY AND UNIFORM CRIME REPORTS

The National Crime Survey (NCS), conducted annually by the Bureau of Justice Statistics (BJS), Department of Justice, interviews 60,000 households to determine how many persons in the United States have been the victims of violent crime. Although it is not specifically aimed at measuring spouse abuse and family violence, because interviewees are asked about their relationship with their attacker, these data include crimes by spouses or ex-spouses. The BJS warns that these data cannot be used as estimates of the true level of spousal violence but are simply estimates of spousal violence that people perceive to be of a criminal nature and are willing or able to report to NCS interviewers. Approximately 56 percent of victimizations (by strangers or intimates) were reported to the police.

According to a special BJS report published in 1991, between 1979 and 1987 an annual average of 427,200 women believed themselves to be victims of a violent crime (rape, robbery, or assault) by a relative. Of that number, 273,000 (64 percent) were victimized by a spouse or ex-spouse. In addition, 198,800 experienced violence by boyfriends. About 79 percent of the spouse abuse cases involved divorced or separated persons, but it is not known whether the incidents occurred before or after divorce or separation.

Black women experienced violence at a rate higher than women of all other races, and Hispanic women experienced more violence than non-Hispanic women. Women aged 16-24 experienced the highest rate of criminal attacks. Separated or divorced women were

CONSTANT FEAR

From its biggest cities to its smallest towns, the United States is an increasingly violent place to be a woman – one of the most violent in the world. Exactly how violent is hard to measure. In the official census of crime in this country, the FBI tracks rape, but not domestic violence. Once every 15 seconds in the United States a woman is beaten by her husband or boyfriend.

Pam Naples, "Battered Women Live Lives of Constant Fear," **Dallas Morning News,** June, 1993

4 1/2 times more likely to be victims of violence than married women. White women were more likely to be assaulted by spouses or ex-spouses and black women were more likely to be assaulted by boyfriends and ex-boyfriends.

As with the NCS, the FBI Uniform Crime Reports (UCR) does not reflect the actual incidence of crime. It presents the number of crimes that are officially reported and recorded by police. According to the UCR, among all female murder victims in 1989, 28 percent (1440) were slain by husbands or boyfriends. Five percent (817) of the male victims were killed by wives or girlfriends.

EXAMINING SEXIST STEREOTYPES

Feminist groups believe women are constantly portrayed in stereotyped ways. Increasingly women have become more concerned with the limiting and/or negative portrayal of themselves by the media. They feel the following images of women in various types of media are harmful and should be eradicated.

- *Media that depict violence as glamorous and exciting, thereby encouraging violence against women as a desirable act.*

- *Images that glamorize the use of children as sexual objects, and teach men that child sexual abuse, incest and prostitution are acceptable forms of entertainment.*

- *Portrayals that reinforce and encourage stereotypic and degrading images of women of color, thereby preventing them from pursuing their individual goals and life potentials.*

- *Images that encourage women not to accept their bodies as they are but to try to change themselves in order to conform to our society's view of beauty. (i.e., weight loss, cosmetics, etc.)*

- *Portrayals of working women as sexual objects to the exclusion of their skills and capabilities. (i.e., airline attendants, etc.)*

- *Media that encourage young women to escape aging at any cost; and further encourage women to feel badly about growing older and reinforce our culture's negative attitudes towards older people.*

- *Images that cause women to feel "less-than" their male counterparts, both physically and mentally.*

Guidelines

1. Examine each statement above that describes a negative image and/or stereotype of women. Do you agree or disagree with the

message of each statement? Why or why not?

2. Think about photos of women in advertising you have seen in magazines and newspapers. Do any of the stereotypes mentioned above apply to these photos?

3. Try to locate examples of negative portrayals of women in magazines and newspapers.

CHAPTER 2

GENDER BASED CRIME AND
THE VIOLENCE AGAINST WOMEN ACT

13. THE RIGHT RESPONSE TO RAPE   67
    Senate Judiciary Committee

14. THE WRONG RESPONSE TO RAPE   74
    Neil Gilbert

15. RAPE IS A GENDER BASED CRIME   80
    Kristian Miccio

16. RAPE IS NOT GENDER BASED   85
    Alan H. Levy

17. FEMINISTS ARE TO BLAME FOR   90
    ANTI-WOMEN VIOLENCE
    Don Feder

18. MEN ARE RESPONSIBLE FOR   94
    GENDER VIOLENCE
    Susan J. Berkson

INTERPRETING EDITORIAL CARTOONS   99
    Reasoning Skill Activity

13   GENDER BASED CRIME AND THE VIOLENCE AGAINST WOMEN ACT

THE RIGHT RESPONSE TO RAPE

Senate Judiciary Committee

The following article is an excerpt from a Senate Judiciary Report titled "The Violence Against Women Act of 1993".

Points to Consider:

1. How effective has the criminal justice system been in prosecuting the perpetrator of a sexual assault?

2. What limitation might Title III have in protecting women from gender-based crime?

3. How might gender-motivated crime be viewed as bias crime?

4. How is the Violence Against Women Act a civil rights remedy to gender-based crime?

Excerpted from a report, " The Violence Against Women Act of 1993" by the U.S. Senate Judiciary Committee, September 7, 1992.

***Most importantly, the act provides, for the first time, a
Federal civil rights remedy aimed at violent gender-
based crimes.***

Senator Biden first introduced the Violence Against Women Act in
1990 in response to the escalating problem of violence against
women. Perhaps the greatest threat to our Nation is the increasing
problem of violent crime that afflicts all people: men, women,
young, and old. Women in America suffer all the crimes that
plague the Nation – muggings, car thefts, and burglaries, to name a
few. But there are also some crimes, including rape and family violence, that disproportionately burden women. Violence against
women reflects as much a failure of our Nation's collective willingness to confront the problem as it does the failure of the Nation's
laws and regulations. Both our resolve and our laws must change if
women are to lead free and equal lives.

The statistics show how far we are from that goal: In 1991, at
least 21,000 domestic crimes were reported to the police every
week; at least 1.1 million reported assaults – including aggravated
assaults, rapes, and murders – were committed against women in
their homes that year; unreported domestic crimes have been estimated to be more than three times this total.

Every week, during 1991, more than 2,000 women were raped,
and more than 90 women were murdered – 9 out of 10 by men.
Women are six times more likely than men to be the victim of a violent crime committed by an intimate; estimates indicate that more
than one of every six sexual assaults is committed by a family member.

Violence is the leading cause of injuries to women ages 15 to 44,
more common than automobile accidents, muggings, and cancer
deaths combined. As many as four million women a year are the
victims of domestic violence. Three out of four women will be the
victim of a violent crime sometime during their life.

Our laws, policies, and attitudes remain inadequate in the face of
the epidemic of violence against women. We live in a country
where:

There are three times as many animal shelters as battered wom-
en's shelters. Almost one-quarter of convicted rapists never go to
prison and another quarter receive sentences in local jails where the
average sentence is 11 months. A recent survey of teenagers

showed high levels of approval of violence: almost 10 percent of the students surveyed said they approved of a husband hitting his wife "if she would not listen to reason"; and more than 12 percent approved of a wife hitting a husband in a similar situation.

The Violence Against Women Act provides, for the first time, a Federal civil rights remedy aimed at violent gender-based crimes. It is time for attacks motivated by gender bias to be considered as serious as crimes motivated by religious, racial, or political bias. The provision's purpose is to provide an effective anti-discrimination remedy for violently expressed gender prejudice. . .

THE VIOLENCE AGAINST WOMEN ACT

The Violence Against Women Act represents an essential step in forging a national consensus that our society will not tolerate violence against women. The act recognizes that many women fear for their safety whether they are at home, on the street, or at school. Women are at risk from those who know them and from those who do not.

But nowhere is the habit of violence harder to break than in the home. Until the 20th century, our society effectively condoned family violence, following a common-law rule known as the "rule of thumb", which barred a husband from "restraining a wife of her liberty by chastisement with a stick thicker than a man's thumb." This rule, originally intended to protect women from excessive violence, in fact led to a reluctance on the part of government to interfere to protect women even where serious violence occurred.

The legacy of societal acceptance of family violence endures even today. In cases where a comparable assault by a stranger on the street would lead to a lengthy jail term, a similar assault by a spouse will result neither in arrest nor in prosecution. For example, a 1989 study in Washington, D.C., found that in over 85 percent of the family violence cases where a woman was found bleeding from wounds, police did not arrest her abuser. Moreover, family violence accounts for a significant number of murders in this country. One-third of all women who are murdered die at the hands of a husband or boyfriend.

National reporting agencies confirm the serious nature of this violence. According to the U.S. Department of Justice, one-third of domestic attacks, if reported, would be classified as felony rapes, robberies, or aggravated assaults. Of the remaining two-thirds classified as simple assaults, almost one-half involved "bodily injury at least as serious as the injury inflicted in 90 percent of all robberies and aggravated assaults.

THE PRICE OF VIOLENCE

Our society pays a heavy price for this violence: one million women a year seek medical attention for injuries caused by violence at the hands of a male partner; children in homes with family violence are 15 times more likely to be abused or neglected than children in peaceful homes; and finally, estimates suggest that we spend $5 to $10 billion a year on health care, criminal justice, and other social costs of domestic violence. Indeed, for the past four years, the U.S. Surgeons General have warned that family violence – not heart attacks or cancer or strokes – poses the single largest threat of injury to adult women in this country.

Unfortunately, the response of the legal system to crimes against women has remained inadequate. A few States still fail to recognize rape of a spouse as a criminal act; other States do not prosecute husbands for rape unless a wife suffers "additional degrees of violence like kidnapping or being threatened with a weapon;" others classify rape of a spouse as a less serious crime with lesser penalties.

Outside the family violence arena, victims of rape are often unable to find either justice or protection in the criminal justice system. From the initial report to the police through prosecution, trial, and sentencing, crimes against women are often treated differently and less seriously that other crimes. Police may refuse to take reports; prosecutors may encourage defendants to plead to minor offenses; judges may rule against victims on evidentiary matters; and juries too often focus on the behavior of the survivors - laying blame on the victims instead of on the attackers. At every step of the way, the criminal justice system poses significant hurdles for victims of sexual assault.

A look at the numbers is telling: over 60 percent of rape reports do not result in arrests; and a rape case is more than twice as likely to be dismissed as a murder case and nearly 40 percent more likely to be dismissed than a robbery case. Less than half of the individuals arrested for rape are convicted of rape. In comparison, 69 percent of those arrested for murder are convicted of murder, and 61 percent of those arrested for robbery are convicted of robbery. Finally, over one-half of all convicted rapists serve an average of only 1 year or less in prison...

THE CIVIL RIGHTS REMEDY – PROTECTION AGAINST VIOLENT GENDER-BASED DISCRIMINATION

Because many questions have been raised regarding Title III of the Violence Against Women Act, this section provides a discussion of the committee's purpose in creating a civil rights remedy for gender-motivated violent crimes, as well as a discussion of the scope of the cause of action authorized by this title.

Title III provides the first Federal civil rights remedy for gender-based violent crimes, allowing any victim of such a crime to bring a civil action against her attacker in Federal court for damages and other relief. Congress has the power to recognize that violence motivated by gender bias "is not merely an individual crime or a personal injury, but is a form of discrimination." With the passage of Title VII of the Civil Rights Act of 1964 (42 U.S.C. 2000e), Congress recognized an important Federal interest in battling gender discrimination and acted to bar that discrimination in the workplace. The Violence Against Women Act recognizes that gender discrimination may take the form not only of a lost pay raise or promotion, but also a violent, criminal attack.

THE PURPOSE: A CIVIL RIGHTS REMEDY FOR GENDER-MOTIVATED CRIMES

Over a century ago, society declared that it would not tolerate attacks against persons because of their race, religion, or national origin. Congress passed the first civil rights laws barring such discrimination in 1871. Traditional civil remedies against violent discrimination, however, have been largely unavailable to victims of gender-based attacks.

More recent legislation has not filled the "gender gap" left by traditional anti-bias crime laws. In the past 10 years, almost every State has passed laws that increase criminal penalties, some of which also provide civil remedies for the victims of hate crimes, but less than a dozen cover gender bias. In 1990, the Congress passed the Hate Crimes Statistics Act, requiring the collection of statistics on crimes motivated by race, ethnicity, national origin, and sexual orientation. Gender-motivated crimes were not mentioned.

The Violence Against Women Act aims to consider gender-motivated bias crimes as seriously as other bias crimes. Whether the attack is motivated by racial bias, ethnic bias, or gender bias, the results are often the same. The victims of such violence are reduced to symbols of hatred; they are chosen not because of who they are as individuals but because of their class status. The violence not only wounds physically, it degrades and terrorizes, instilling fear and inhibiting the lives of all those similarly situated. "Placing this violence in the context of the civil rights laws recognizes it for what it is – a hate crime."

Given the failure of recent legislative proposals to recognize gender-motivated crime, it is especially important to acknowledge its discriminatory dimensions now. As Illinois Attorney General Roland Burris testified before the committee: "Until women as a class have the same protection offered others who are objects of irrational, hate-motivated abuse and assault, we as a society should feel humiliated and ashamed..."

THE SCOPE OF THE ACT IS LIMITED TO GENDER-MOTIVATED, NOT RANDOM, CRIMES

To satisfy the burden of establishing a civil rights cause of action, the plaintiff must prove that the defendant's act was motivated by gender bias. This civil rights cause of action is no different than the cause of action an African-American might use. For example, an African-American man or woman who is the victim of an assault, cannot under our present laws say, "My civil rights were violated because I am an African-American and someone that wasn't

72

African-American did me harm." He or she must prove racial animus.

Similarly, a woman who is attacked and seeks relief under Title III must demonstrate that the defendant attacked her because she is a woman and that the attacker was motivated, at least in part, by her gender. For example, she might offer proof that a defendant entered a department store carrying a gun, picked out women in the store and shot her while screaming anti-women epithets, and leaving the many nearby men unharmed. The fact that the attacker had in this example verbally expressed his bias against women is helpful, but not mandatory. The fact that the attacker segregated the men from the women and then shot only the women might be evidence enough of his gender-based motivation.

14 GENDER BASED CRIME AND THE VIOLENCE AGAINST WOMEN ACT

THE WRONG RESPONSE TO RAPE

Neil Gilbert

Neil Gilbert is a professor of social welfare at the University of California at Berkeley. The following article appeared in The Wall Street Journal.

Points to Consider:

1. Cite evidence from this reading that rape victims do receive equal justice compared with other crime victims.

2. Evaluate the claim that more rapes go unreported than other crimes.

3. What trend in the rate of rape does the BJS study show?

4. What argument is there against making rape a civil offense?

Neil Gilbert, "The Wrong Response to Rape," **The Wall Street Journal,** June 29, 1993. Reprinted by permission.

The act is designed to promote the cause of radical feminists, whose exaggerated claims of victimization deserve the critical scrutiny they are just beginning to receive from moderate feminists.

The Senate Judiciary Committee has answered the dreams of radical feminist lawyers with its proposed Violence Against Women Act of 1993, which would classify rape motivated by gender bias as a civil rights offense under which victims could sue for compensatory and punitive damages. The act also earmarks $85 million to rape crisis centers for education and prevention services to deal with an epidemic of date rape that does not really exist, but is likely to be spawned by linking rape to civil rights and punitive damages.

The argument for making rape a civil rights offense and granting millions to rape crisis centers is detailed in the Judiciary Committee's majority staff report, "The Response to Rape: Detours on the Road to Equal Justice." As the title suggests, the staff's analysis charges that rape victims do not receive equal justice under the current law. Their case rests on findings of inequality between rape and other violent crimes related to rates of convictions, dismissals and reporting. Following the tendency of most documents that advocate for a cause, this report furnishes a highly one-sided reading of the evidence, relying on vivid anecdotes to support fragile numbers.

Two of the principal claims, repeated several times throughout the report, are that 84% of reported rapes never result in a conviction and that in 88% of reported rapes the assailant is not incarcerated. We are also informed that while less than half of all individuals arrested for rape are convicted, more than 60% of those arrested for robbery are convicted. All this is true. Whether it reflects unequal justice is another matter.

THE NUMBERS IN PERSPECTIVE

What the report does not tell us is that, using exactly the same computations on the data from the same sources, 87% of reported robberies never result in a conviction and in 89% of reported robberies the assailant is not incarcerated. The overall conviction rates are roughly the same for aggravated assault and somewhat lower for the nonviolent crime of burglary. Although the report provides only the numbers that intimate an alarming inequality of justice, the fact is that among the violent crimes of rape, robbery and aggravated assault, the relation between reported crimes and convictions is equally deplorable.

Compared with the data on reported cases of robbery, the data on reported rapes reveals both a higher percentage of arrests and a higher percentage of dismissals before coming to trial. Dismissals before trial are commonly the result of weak evidence or the victim's refusal to testify. According to the staff's analysis, however, "in rape cases there is another factor at work." That is, the victims are often acquainted with their molesters.

The report cites evidence that prosecutors hesitate to bring any case to trial – whether it be a robbery case, an assault case, or a kidnapping case – in which the offender knew the victim. In light of this tendency, the report speculates that proportionately more rapes (48%) than robberies (37%) are dismissed not because the evidence might have been weak or because the victims decided not to testify, but because in a very high proportion of reported cases the offender was not a stranger.

RAPE VICTIMS

It is true that many victims of rape know their assailants, but so do the victims of other violent crimes (a point the report fails to convey). Indeed, according to the Bureau of Justice Statistics figures for 1989 and 1990, the proportion of victims reporting robberies and aggravated assaults who were acquainted with their offenders was as high as – if not higher than – those for reported rapes. Although dismissal rates vary, once the cases make it to the courtroom the conviction rates for rape and robbery are almost equal.

Finally, claims about unequal rates of arrest and convictions for rapists are magnified by the issue of unreported cases. Another reflection of what is said to be the unequal justice afforded women is the fact that many, if not most, rapes go unreported. No one really knows the number of these unreported cases. But we are informed by the Judiciary Committee staff that "according to the conservative estimates, as many as 84% of rapes each year are never reported." They explain in a footnote that this estimate is "conservative" when compared with figures presented by University of Arizona Prof. Mary Koss, who directed the *Ms. Magazine* Campus Project on Sexual Assault.

Prof. Koss's widely publicized figures showed that 27% of college women were victims of rape or attempted rape an average of two

Lead with your strongest suit.

INTIMIDATION APPAREL
Tempered Steel
For the woman who means business.
NEW YORK   CHICAGO   PARIS

Cartoon by Carol & Simpson. Reprinted with permission.

times between the ages of 14 and 21. The problem with this study is that 73% of the college women whom Prof. Koss classified as victims did not think they had been raped; more than 40% went back and had sex again with the man who Prof. Koss believed raped them. Most of the college women in Prof. Koss's study probably counted themselves as feminists, but to the radical fringe they are rape victims who (like the male targets of fringe criticism) "just don't get it." Next to this study, almost any research on rape looks conservative.

THE PROBLEM

There are several problems with the so-called conservative estimate of unreported rapes drawn by the Judiciary Committee staff from a study entitled "Rape in America," conducted by the National Victim Center and the Crime Victims Research and Treatment Center. Based on the results of a national survey, the study estimates that 683,000 women are victims of rape each year. The survey sample was scientifically designed to allow for valid generalizations to the broader population. But the accuracy of these generalizations is seriously undermined by the fact that almost one-third of the scientifically designed sample did not participate in the second wave of interviews, from which the annual incidence rate of rape was calculated.

The 3,220 study participants interviewed during the second wave amounted to only 68% of the original sample. With a sample this size, the nationwide estimate of 683,000 rapes was based on 23 cases of rape uncovered in the interviews.

For a truly conservative estimate of unreported rape cases the Judiciary Committee staff could have turned to the findings of the Bureau of Justice Statistics surveys, actually conducted by the Census Bureau, which involve a random sample of about 62,000 households interviewed every six months, with response rates of more than 90%. The BJS findings reveal that in 1989 and 1990 almost half of their respondents who were victims of rape did not report this crime to the police. Although this figure is lower than the 84% of unreported cases cited in the Judiciary Committee's staff report, it is no trivial matter. Once again, however, on this score rape victims do not differ from victims of other violent crimes. According to the BJS data, 49% of robbery cases and 43% of aggravated assault cases were not reported to the police during this period.

The BJS studies, of course, are not free of methodological problems. They have been widely criticized for underestimating the incidence of rape. But as Christopher Jencks notes, since the BJS surveys are conducted almost the same way every year, their biases are likely to be constant – so these figures provide a reliable guide to trends in violent crime over time. In this regard it is worth noting that the BJS data show the rate of rape declining about 30% between 1980 and 1990.

INSUFFERABLE NORMS

The good news in all these numbers is that regarding rates of arrest, convictions, dismissals and reportings, victims of rape are not treated any less equally that other crime victims. Despite the claims in the Judiciary Committee's staff report, the evidence does not demonstrate a "consistent pattern that diverges from the norm." The unfortunate news is that justice is appallingly thin all about – for all victims the norms are insufferable.

> ## RAPE LEVELS DECLINE
>
> *Meanwhile, says Biden, "Women are being victimized more and more. And society's doing less and less about it." Never mind Bureau of Justice Statistics that show the incidents of rape per 1,000 women declined 30 percent between 1980 and 1990.*
>
> Ruth Shalit, "Caught in the Act," **The New Republic**, July 12, 1993

But the answer is not to make rape a civil rights offense. This would lower the threshold of proof in rape cases, introduce psychological issues of motivation, and provide a huge financial incentive for expanding the definition of rape (in line with the radical feminist agenda) to include all sorts of ambiguous or unpleasant sexual experiences. The big winners in all this would of course be the lawyers and the therapists. Nor is equal justice advanced by giving rape crisis centers $85 million to combat an epidemic that does not exist.

The act is designed to promote the cause of radical feminists, whose exaggerated claims of victimization deserve the critical scrutiny they are just beginning to receive from moderate feminists. If the Judiciary Committee's aim is to champion the cause of equal justice for all citizens, these funds can be better spent to improve our courts and to increase the number of police protecting our communities.

15   GENDER BASED CRIME AND THE VIOLENCE AGAINST WOMEN ACT

RAPE IS A GENDER BASED CRIME

Kristian Miccio

Kristian Miccio is the founding director of the Sanctuary's Center for Battered Women's Legal Services and chair of the board of the New York City Coalition of Battered Women's Advocates. She is an attorney who specializes in representing women who are victims of gender motivated violence.

Points to Consider:

1. Why should rape be placed in the context of bias-motivated crimes?

2. Explain how rape is a tool of domination.

3. What danger lies in viewing rape as a "crime of passion"?

4. What has been the effect of viewing rape as a "private act"?

Excerpted from testimony by Kristian Miccio before the U.S. House Judiciary Committee, Subcommittee on Crime and Criminal Justice, May 11, 1992.

Rape is the most powerful tool of domination as it functions and operates as a means of social control.

Let me preface my remarks by congratulating you on your wisdom and your courage in proposing legislation that seeks to protect women and men who are victims of violent crime motivated by hatred. One can only hope that your edifying example will be followed by your colleagues in the Congress with the passage of a meaningful hate-crimes bill – one that affords protection to lesbians and gay men and that extends full protection to women.

Hate crimes against women are manifested through acts of sexual and physical violence. Indeed, FBI statistics reveal that gender motivated violence against women, specifically rape and "domestic" violence, is spiralling upward thereby outstripping other forms of crime. In the past ten years rape of women by men rose four times as fast as the national crime rate. Moreover, three to four million women were physically assaulted by their husbands. FBI and Bureau of Justice statistics tell us, quite succinctly, that a woman is raped every six minutes and every 15 seconds a women is beaten.

HATE CRIMES

According to experts such as Dr. Mary Koss from the American Psychological Association, hate crimes against women are neither random nor arbitrary. They are most often perpetrated by men who know or live with their victims. Indeed, the site for such violence is often the home, the school, the dorm room or the office and it is perpetrated by one whom the victim knows and trusts.

Hate crimes against women because we are women is palpably different from bias motivated violence against other classes of individuals. To rape or beat a woman requires little logistical effort – one need not stalk a particular bar or terrorize a particular part of the city to perpetrate this form of violence. Legislation then which purports to protect victims of hate motivated violence must include gender and accommodate this difference.

Rape and the threat of violence based on gender robs women of our freedom and violates our civil rights. It results from the structural relationships of power, of domination and of privilege between men and women in society. It is a political act since it carries with it the same potential for tearing apart the fabric of our society as hate crimes based on race, ethnicity, religion, or sexual orientation.

Furthermore, acts of violence based on gender – like acts of violence based on race, ethnicity, religion and sexual orientation – are not random, isolated crimes against persons who happen to be female. Rather, these are crimes against individuals that are meant to intimidate and terrorize the larger group or class of people – women. This places rape in the context of bias-motivated hated crimes; we are raped because we are female.

DOMINATION

When a man rapes a woman, he sends the same message to all women that a hate crime against a black person sends to all black people. That message is domination and control. Rape is the most powerful tool of domination as it functions and operates as a means of social control. Rape keeps women in a secondary status in society by closing doors, limiting options and opportunities, and denying autonomy and freedom. Violence and the internalized and constant threat of violence permeates every aspect of women's lives. The fear of rape controls what women wear, where we live, where we work and how we behave. Rape, and the fear of rape, places limits on our liberty and our mobility. Indeed, when a woman is attacked for being in a place where men are safe, it is just as much a bias-related crime as the recent racially motivated murders in Bensonhurst and Howard Beach.

CULTURAL MYTHS AND GENDER ROLES

The cultural myth that suggests that rape is a "crime of passion" or a "private act" must be debunked. Such acts are not motivated by passion or provocation, but rather by the hatred, anger and the desire to control a class of individuals – women. Further, the suggestion that acquaintance rape falls outside the ambit of "hate crimes" belies an understanding of the motive behind the act. The argument that the relationship between the victim and the perpetrator is the salient factor assumes the legitimacy of male ownership and domination of women. The notion that violence committed by an acquaintance or partner cannot, by definition, be motivated in major part by women-hating ignores the reality of these crimes against women.

Furthermore, defining rape between intimates as a "private act" reinforces a vicious cycle of violence against women. The "privatization" of rape in the family and the concomitant view of women as chattel led to the cultural acceptance of marital rape. Indeed, up

Cartoon by Steve Sack. Reprinted with permission of the **Star Tribune**, Minneapolis.

until 1984, the state could not prosecute a husband for raping his wife since her status – that of wife – made it legally impossible for her to withhold consent. In 1984, just eight years ago, the New York State Court of Appeals removed the last vestige of cultural misogyny by declaring the marital rape exemption unconstitutional. (See People v. Liberta, 64 N.Y.2d 152.) Now, married women are afforded equal protection under the law.

SUMMARY

Any legislation aimed at hate crimes that fails to include gender sends the not so subtle message that women, and crimes of hate perpetrated against us are inconsequential – that these acts are not "real" hate crimes – a message I am sure neither you nor other members of Congress wish to send to the women of this nation.

Crimes of hate against women are at once invisible and all pervasive in our culture. If you are born female this paradox is difficult to live with. Yet, whenever we as a society attempt to grapple with crimes of hate we never recognize women as a discrete class of victims. Crimes against women, however, occur at epidemic proportions. Indeed, the Surgeon General has stated that violence against women is the chief cause of death and injury to women.

Hate against women is as old as time itself and the patterns of

SEXUAL DOMINATION

Although murder, the ultimate crime of violence, affects both women and men, many murders of women can be seen as the final expression of patriarchal values of sexual domination.... For example, all recorded serial murderers have been men and the large majority kill women (Caputi, 1987); in addition, they frequently bind, rape, and torture their victims before they murder them.

Feminist analysts and activists against violence all insist that violence against women must no longer be defined solely as a crime against an individual who happens to be female and is unfortunate enough to become a victim. Rather, this violence must be seen for what it is – a crime of misogyny, of hatred of women.... The evidence is in the fact that women worldwide "are routinely subject to torture, starvation, terrorism, humiliation, mutilation, and even murder simply because they are female."

Center for Women Policy Studies, "Violence Against Women," May, 1991

hatred are socially ingrained. Notwithstanding this obvious fact, such crimes remain unspoken in our collective discourse. Today, to keep such acts "in the closet" diminishes us all. Therefore, if this body truly wishes to attack all crimes of hate, women must be included. Anything less would be to create the illusion of protection and to render hate crimes against women invisible once again.

16 GENDER BASED CRIME AND THE VIOLENCE AGAINST WOMEN ACT

RAPE IS NOT GENDER BASED

Alan H. Levy

Alan H. Levy, Ph.D. is an Associate Professor of History at George Mason University, Fairfax, Virginia. The following is an excerpt from Levy's testimony before the Senate Judiciary Committee.

Points to Consider:

1. What populations make up the majority of male rape victims?

2. Summarize Susan Brownmiller and Becky Thompson's assertions regarding rape.

3. Why must violence against women be viewed in a humanist rather than feminist framework?

4. Discuss the apparent correlation between rape and other violent crime.

Excerpted from testimony by Alan H. Levy in testimony before the U.S. Senate Judiciary Committee, April 9, 1991.

Violence against women needs to be understood in a humanist context, for a more narrow feminist framework ignores many victims.

While I will present you no systematic, data-laden study on the subject, my findings, albeit impressionistic, from volunteer work with dysfunctional families and with children of alcoholics, reveal that a significant number of males have been the victims of sexual violence in their lives, mostly as young boys. A colleague who runs a rape crisis center in Pittsburgh also told me that in 1987 approximately 40% of the victims who came to her center were males – almost all young boys. I cannot judge whether that statistic is typical, or, for that matter, whether it is accurate, but if it is the least bit valid we have a major, and largely untouched dimension to the whole problem before us. Perhaps the FBI has data on the number of male rape victims. I would guess that, as was the case with women for so many years, and which still remains the case for many, a reluctance to report rape hides the degree of severity of the problem of male victims. In addition to the hidden facts about young males, there are of course the well documented tragedies which occur in prisons. The other factual evidence with which I preface my remarks is highly personal – I was raped when I was eight years old.

THREE POINTS

There are three points I would like to address in regard to the implications of the added dimension of male victims of rape to which I believe your committee ought to give careful consideration:

1) If official reports, as well as journalistic coverage, would give attention to all victims, there may be a reduction in the levity with which some men still regard the topic.

2) Derived from the first point, if males were more aware of rape as a crime of which they can also be potential life-long victims, federal, state, local, and private agencies may be willing to devote more resources than is currently the case. These days many crisis centers are barely managing, and it would indeed be tragic if some closed due to a public indifference.

3) This matter is less significant in my mind than the first two, though it is perhaps more politically sensitive. Rarely have I raised the issue of male victimization in conversations with women and met anything but empathy and understanding. But occasionally I

ESCALATING VIOLENCE

The simplest fact is that rape is a serious problem in America because violent crime is a serious problem in America. The increased rape in the United States is occurring against a backdrop of escalating violence of all kinds: drive-by shootings, mass shootings, gang warfare, various drug violence, random assault, and murder. The level of all violent crime rose 24 percent from 1987 to 1991, according to the FBI; rape rose 13 percent in the same period. As with violent crime in general, rape is much more common in cities than in suburban or rural areas. You won't find much rape in Wyoming or rural Michigan, where people still leave their doors unlocked.

While the United States has one of the highest levels of rape in the world, rape is virtually unknown in countries with low levels of violent crime – a fact that demolishes the feminist arguments about the universal male propensity for rape. The rape rate in the United States is four times higher than Germany's, 13 times higher than England's, and 20 times higher than Japan's. All of these countries have commensurately lower levels of violent crime than the United States.

Margaret D. Bonilla, "Cultural Assault," **Policy Review**, Fall, 1993

have encountered a disturbing radical feminism which seeks, in effect, to use rape to highlight male/female antagonisms. Indeed truly radical feminists going back to Kate Millett assert unresolvable gender antagonisms to be a fixed premise on which analysis of all male/female interaction must be based. For such ideologues rape is a most hideous and basic theme, famously articulated by Susan Brownmiller in *Against Our Will* in which she asserts that all men are potential rapists; all women are victims; and rape is but an exaggeration of what men do to women all the time. Similarly, Becky Thompson wrote in a manual distributed by the American Sociological Association, "I begin with the basic feminist principle that in a... sexist society we have swallowed oppressive ways... it is not open to debate whether a... male is sexist. He simply is." To confound such convictions with the undeniable fact that men too are victims of rape undercuts the premise of these virulent minority views which pervade much discourse over the subject.

From my experience, such ideologues respond to the undeniable dimension of male victimization of rape in manners which range from consternation to laughter to angry dismissal – a similar range to that I have witnessed among the "Bobby Knight" types. Some women have even mockingly asked: "Did you enjoy it?" All such responses involve denial, in some cases indeed in the full psychological sense of the word, of the complete human tragedy of rape. The "Bobby Knights" are pathetic; the "Susan Brownmillers", while not wrong (except in the assertion that all men are rapists), are, however, sadly incomplete. Most listen; many, however, chose to ignore…

HUMANIST CONTEXT

Violence against women needs to be understood in a humanist context, for a more narrow feminist framework ignores many victims. This is an ignorance which is distorting, alienating, and dangerously empowering in its effects. In parallel, treatment of domestic violence reveals similar pitfalls, for many of the victims here are also male, and they are totally ignored. Again, this neither negates nor diminishes such horrors women face. But it does compel everyone to face the tragic but unavoidable fact that all people are potential victims, and that the proclivity toward violence is not the purview of one gender. Indeed *Ms. Magazine* has recently touched upon the growing, heretofore closeted problem of domestic violence within some lesbian households. Tendencies toward violence may manifest themselves in different forms in men and women, but neither is immune. (And indeed males and females appear equally prone to child abuse.) But we allow the false notion of gender immunity to color our treatment of issues like rape. Hence to some victims – males – the message is: your pain is not real, or at least it does not warrant much political attention…

A still largely male power structure accepts the assertion of some feminists that they legitimately hold 100% of the claim on victimization here. The exchange between the politically powerful and the officially recognized victims soothes the powerful who can then congratulate themselves that they have acted humanely, which they have, but not as completely as they could. Meanwhile all other victims are ignored, the politically acceptable victims have, with the utmost of self-entitlement, drowned them. These officially recognized victims then suppress any subsequent questioning of the arrangement as that which does not fit the party line.

And with respect to Becky Thompson's views that all men are sex-

88

ists, how can such views do anything but exacerbate hatreds? Yet they are indulged by many in positions of institutional power for fear of outraging those who will speak loudly. The likes of Al Sharpton and Susan Brownmiller need then to be ignored. Their sense of their own immunity exacerbates the hatred they hold. Rejecting them takes courage, the courage to see politics as more than a mere matter of placating the noisiest constituencies. Let us keep the likes of Martin Luther King and Betty Friedan at the forefront and face all such problems in their fullest human context. Otherwise they will simply keep coming back, not despite our good efforts but paradoxically because of them.

FEMALE VICTIMIZATION

The incompleteness inherent in casting rape exclusively as a matter of female victimization can too easily enter into official reports and journalistic coverage. There is no question that women must live with far greater fears of rape than men, wherever they work, walk, jog... But there remain men who must live with ghosts that can be just as debilitating; of that I can personally assure you.

Any addressing of the issue of rape ought never divide humans on the basis of gender; it ought always seek to unite. We often say rape has nothing to do with sex; it is a crime of violence and degradation. Let that fact never be diluted or distorted by an incomplete reporting of the victims.

17   GENDER BASED CRIME AND THE VIOLENCE AGAINST WOMEN ACT

FEMINISTS ARE TO BLAME FOR ANTI-WOMEN VIOLENCE

Don Feder

Don Feder is a nationally syndicated conservative journalist. His articles often appear in The Conservative Chronicle.

Points to Consider:

1. Contrast characteristics of rape-prone and rape-free societies according to Hood. Does the theory hold?

2. Summarize the "feminist agenda".

3. What is the "demystification of femininity"? How has it encouraged crimes against women?

4. Restate Gilder's contention regarding sex distinction.

The feminist agenda has triumphed. A majority of
women now work outside the home.

The feminist response to the rising rate of crime against women is to pour kerosene on a social conflagration. In an anti-Father's Day celebration, a group of feminists gathered on the Boston Common to oppose "patriarchal violence against women and children." "Rage, battering, and incest are the holy trinity of patriarchy," organizer Gail Dines informed ladies carrying signs inscribed "Mad at Dad" and "Father Doesn't Know Best". It's easy to dismiss the protesters as the lunatic fringe of women's lib. But their message – hatred of men, the conviction that rape and assault are a reflection of masculinity – permeates the movement.

WILDING

In an opinion piece in the *New York Times* commenting on the Central Park "wilding" incident, in which a young executive was savagely beaten and gang-raped by six teens, Jane C. Hood indicates our definition of gender. "In a society that equates masculinity with dominance, and sex with violence, gang rape becomes a way for adolescents to prove their masculinity both to themselves and to each other," the University of New Mexico sociologist observes.

Hood contrasts the differences between what she terms rape-prone and rape-free societies. The former are associated with "militarism, interpersonal violence in general, and an ideology of male toughness." The latter "encourage female participation in the economy and political system, and male involvement in child rearing."

Her solutions include an all-out attack on gender inequality in the workplace, resistance to parental-leave policies, and war toys. She favors promoting more male involvement in day care, the extension of sex education, and co-ed sports.

GENDER CRIMES

Hood conveniently neglects to identify these so-called rape-prone and rape-free cultures. International crime statistics, compiled by Interpol, leave one perplexed. Sweden, which comes closest to approximating the feminist ideal of a uni-sex milieu, has four times more rapes per hundred thousand inhabitants than Mexico, the land that gave macho its name. In Saudi Arabia, where women are cloistered, and a glimpse of stocking is considered a capital offense, sexual assault is nearly nonexistent. Those who tout the theory that tra-

News Item: WOMEN'S POWDER ROOM INSTALLED IN SENATE CHAMBERS.

Cartoon by Jim Borgman. Reprinted with special permission of King Features Syndicate.

ditional relationships promote crimes against women are left with an uncomfortable question: If gender differentiation stimulates sex crimes, why are we experiencing far more of these offenses today than a generation ago?

The feminist agenda has triumphed. A majority of women now work outside the home. There are severe legal constraints against discrimination in the work place. Women are invading what once were all-male bastions. Normative sex roles are out of fashion, and the dogma that the sexes are psychologically identical is widely accepted. Yet crimes against women are on an upward spiral.

THE FOUNDATION

In fact, feminists laid the foundation of the Central Park ethos. They were early advocates of no-fault divorce. If marriage was bondage, divorce was emancipation, they reasoned, losing no opportunity to denigrate wedlock and homemaking. "Being a housewife is an illegitimate profession," feminist author Vivian Gornick proclaimed. Said Andrea Dworkin of Women Against Pornography, "Rape is the first model of marriage."

The wind was sown in the Sixties, the whirlwind reaped in the Eighties and beyond. Violence between partners and child abuse – sexual as well as physical – all are far more prevalent in families

92

EXAGGERATED CONTROVERSY

Some women want to see men walking around in a perpetual state of terror, afraid to make eye contact, weighing each word before it's spoken (to assure it's innuendo-free and couldn't possibly be misinterpreted), flattening themselves against a wall when a woman passes them in a corridor, lest shoulders brush inadvertently.

It's the feminist way of punishing men for everything from diapers to date rape, and establishing gender superiority... Normal women treat this exaggerated controversy with the contempt it deserves. They don't feel abused, oppressed or exploited. They don't hate their nature. They don't nurture a gender grudge the size of Mt. Rushmore. They generally like men.

Don Feder, "Harassment Charges Used to Intimidate," **Creators Syndicate, Inc.**, 1991

where the divorced, or never-married mom has a live-in boyfriend (which is increasingly the case).

Boys reared in households without a permanent male member who is committed to the family, rarely see loving interaction between the sexes and lack healthy role models. From the conduct of companions toward their mothers, many learn to view women as objects of exploitation.

The demystification of femininity also has aided the process. When women were cast down from the pedestal, at the behest of feminists, decline of respect for their gender soon followed. George Gilder, who dealt with these issues in his seminal work *Work and Marriage*, contends: "Boys need separate areas in which to establish themselves. If you destroy these distinctions, they are left with the lowest common denominator of sexuality: their superior strength and aggressiveness." Thus they distinguish themselves by being more violent, more phallic.

Don't blame patriarchy for the sins of its detractors. Feminists, look around you. If the social perspective is appalling, remember, sisters, you asked for it.

18   GENDER BASED CRIME AND THE VIOLENCE AGAINST WOMEN ACT

MEN ARE RESPONSIBLE FOR GENDER VIOLENCE

Susan J. Berkson

Susan J. Berkson, a resident of Saint Paul, wrote the following article which appeared in the Star Tribune *of Minneapolis.*

Points to Consider:

1. Summarize statistics from the FBI's 1990 Uniform Crime Report.

2. Analyze: "We see black. We see white. We do not see gender."

3. Explain: "The only thing rapists have in common is their gender."

4. How might the United States be regarded as "Two Nations"?

Susan J. Berkson, " To Get at the Roots of Violence, the Relevant Factor Is Gender," **Star Tribune**, June 18, 1992. Reprinted by permission of the **Star Tribune**, Minneapolis.

According to FBI 1990 Uniform Crime Reports, 81.6 percent of all crimes are committed by men, almost 89 percent of violent crimes are committed by men, and 90 percent of all homicides are committed by men.

See no gender. Hear no gender. Speak no gender. If the gender is male. Just like the three monkeys who see no evil, hear no evil, and speak no evil, so are we with gender (unless the gender is female).

Last week, a friend speculated as to the color of the murderers of the two St. Paul convenience store clerks. This was on a night when the news also included reports on the alleged kidnapper of Corrine Erstad, the continuing search for the assailant of Miranda Paffel, and an update on Aquisha Smith, the 8-year-old girl who four years ago was raped, beaten and left for dead in a dumpster.

A VIOLENT AMERICA

Oh, why is this country so violent, we moan. What's wrong with Americans, we lament. Wrong questions. We should be asking, why are men in this country so violent: What's wrong with American men?

Now, before you jump out of your seat and scream that not all men are violent, that there's nothing wrong with American men, stop the "man-bashing", look at these statistics from the very manly FBI. According to their 1990 Uniform Crime Reports, 81.6 percent of all crimes are committed by men, almost 89 percent of violent crimes are committed by men, and 90 percent of all homicides are committed by men.

This is not just the majority, but the vast majority, the overwhelming majority. Whenever one demographic group – whether delineated by color, economic status, national origin, or female gender – is a clear lopsided majority, we hear about it. But if that lopsided majority is male, we don't even see it.

See no gender. Hear no gender. Speak no gender.

DISCRIMINATION

See it — because not everything in this country can be explained in black and white. The role of race and by default, racism, in this country cannot be minimized. Neither, in a country that refuses to

Cartoon by Steve Sack. Reprinted with permission of the **Star Tribune**, Minneapolis.

guarantee to women equal rights in its constitution, can the role of gender.

This is a country where women are still second-class citizens, regardless of their color or economic status. While Congress and the courts have extended some civil rights legislation to include women, de facto sexism is rampant. The Senate is still 98 percent male. (Some representative government!) Zero percent of the presidents and vice presidents have been women. Women earn only 73 cents to a man's dollar. This is a country where 684,000 women were raped last year, where one out of four women will be raped in her lifetime. (Greatest country in the world!" says George Bush.)

Who's doing the bashing? I know it's not you. It's not me. It's not "Thelma & Louise".

Who beat Rodney King?

Who beat truck driver Reginald Denny?

Who were the vast majority of the 15,008 arrested for rioting in Los Angeles County?

We see black. We see white. We do not see gender.

GANG RAPES

On March 8, Mexico City witnessed the largest International Women's Day march in the country's history. Some 20,000 women in 46 contingents accompanied by a giant woman puppet danced, threw confetti, chanted and spray-painted calls for an end to violence against women.

The unprecedented level of participation and of official vigilance resulted from both a rise in women's organizing and to the central demand of the march – the call for the resignation of the attorney general in charge of Mexico's "war on drugs", Javier Coello Trejo. The women were angered by his cover-up of 19 reported gang rapes committed, according to victim identification, by members of his personal staff.

Elaine Burns, "Mexican Women Protest Official Rape," **Guardian**, March 21, 1990

GENDER VIOLENCE

If the police officers who beat Rodney King had been women, the subject of the analyses would have been "Women: Fit to be cops?" If women had pulled Denny from his truck and beat him, the columnists would be asking, "What's wrong with women?" If women had been out on the streets shooting guns and beating motorists, *Time* and *Newsweek* would run cover stories on "Killer Women: The Phenomenon of Female Violence." But the perpetrators were male, so their gender went unmentioned.

We see black. We see white. We do not see gender. After their post-Rodney King verdict meeting with President Bush, civil rights leaders told the press that in order for the crisis to be solved, unemployment and poverty had to be eliminated.

Men with jobs don't rape? Men with money don't batter? In 1990, *Newsweek* reported that rape crosses so many lines that no single profile fits all rapists. The only thing rapists have in common is their gender. "We have all types," reported an Atlanta police detective, "from cut-off jeans to pinstripe suits, from those who live in ghettos to those who work in boardrooms." A study by the National Institute of Mental Health found that battering, as well, cuts across all lines of color and economic status.

Women are angry. Women are unemployed, are mired in poverty, have despair. Women have lots of rage at men and at a system that oppresses them. By and large, however, women do not batter, rape, or go into the street and shoot men.

More attention might be paid if they did. Look at the uproar caused by two fictional characters (Thelma and Louise) who acted on their anger and shot a sexist, abusive man. "Man-bashing," the male critics cried. And a real woman is physically bashed every 15 seconds. These are not women's problems. These are men's problems.

TWO NATIONS

The *St. Paul Pioneer Press* recently ran excerpts from *Two Nations*, a book examining the politics of race. The book might have been about the politics of gender, because there are also two nations for the sexes: one United States for men (they earn more, have more opportunities, more career options, fewer child-rearing and domestic responsibilities, more freedom to travel, more freedom to procreate), a second United States for women (they earn less, have fewer opportunities, fewer career options, more child-rearing and domestic responsibilities, less freedom to travel, less freedom to procreate, more likely to be demeaned, dismissed, scorned, sexually harassed, raped, and battered). Separate. Nowhere near equal.

Racism is abhorrent. Its impact is not to be minimized. But as we continue our discussions about what happened in Los Angeles and what needs to change in this country, we need to consider the role of gender. Without it we cannot get a full picture. Without a full picture, we cannot find a full solution. All seven of those charged with the murders of the convenience store clerks are male.

INTERPRETING EDITORIAL CARTOONS

This activity may be used as an individualized study guide for students in libraries and resource centers or as a discussion catalyst in small group and classroom discussions.

Although cartoons are usually humorous, the main intent of most political cartoonists is not to entertain. Cartoons express serious social comment about important issues. Using graphic and visual arts, the cartoonist expresses opinions and attitudes. By employing an entertaining and often light-hearted visual format, cartoonists may have as much or more impact on national and world issues as editorial and syndicated columnists.

Points to Consider

1. Examine the cartoon on the next page.

2. How would you describe the message of the cartoon? Try to describe the message in one to three sentences.

3. Do you agree with the message expressed in the cartoon? Why or why not?

4. Does the cartoon support the author's point of view in any of the readings in this publication? If the answer is yes, be specific about which reading or readings and why.

5. Are any of the readings in Chapter Two in basic agreement with the cartoon?

Cartoon by Craig MacIntosh. Reprinted with permission of the **Star Tribune**, Minneapolis.

CHAPTER 3

CONTROLLING SEXUAL OFFENDERS

19. SEXUAL PREDATORS AND PRISON   102
    TERMS: AN OVERVIEW
       Bill Richards

20. TREATING SEXUAL OFFENDERS: 109
    THE POINT
       Andrew Vachss

21. TREATING SEXUAL OFFENDERS: 114
    THE COUNTERPOINT
       Task Force on Sexual Violence

22. AN ARGUMENT AGAINST PREVENTIVE   119
    DETENTION
       Minnesota Civil Liberties Union

23. IN SUPPORT OF PREVENTIVE DETENTION   123
       State of Minnesota

WHAT IS SEX BIAS?   128
    Reasoning Skill Activity

19   CONTROLLING SEXUAL OFFENDERS

SEXUAL PREDATORS AND PRISON TERMS: AN OVERVIEW

Bill Richards

Bill Richards is a staff reporter for The Wall Street Journal.

Points to Consider:

1. What is Washington's "Sexual Predator" law?

2. Summarize criticisms of the Predator Law.

3. Define preventive detention.

While it has drawn praise from victims' rights groups, Washington's predator law is raising some troubling and complex questions for many legal experts.

Five months after finishing up his sentence for rape, Vance Cunningham looked like a prison success story. Mr. Cuningham had his high-school equivalency diploma, a promising job as a mechanic on a fishing boat and, most important, a clean bill of health from a prison psychologist.

But Washington's End-of-Sentence Review Committee thought otherwise. Scanning the records of sex offenders, the 10-member panel took note of Mr. Cunningham's history: convictions for three rapes and an arrest as a juvenile for demanding oral sex from an adult woman at knifepoint.

Mr. Cunningham's past, the committee concluded, looked too risky to warrant taking chances with his future. It invoked Washington's "Sexual Predator" law, the only statute of its kind in the nation. The law, enacted in the wake of a sensational 1989 child mutilation case, permits the state to lock up indefinitely any convicted violent sex offender – after he has served his time. Since it was passed, Washington has confirmed 15 "predators", including Mr. Cunningham. None has been charged with or even suspected of committing a new crime. Instead, the state contends the men's criminal histories demonstrate that they have a "mental abnormality" requiring confinement until they can be successfully treated.

WHAT IS "ABNORMAL"?

One catch: psychiatry has no clinical definition for "mental abnormality." Thus, there is no way technically to cure a detainee. "It will be some time before these guys get out," agrees David Boerner, who wrote the predator statute. "Old age or some kind of technological breakthrough might do it."

While it has drawn praise from victims' rights groups, Washington's predator law is raising some troubling and complex questions for many legal and medical experts. Critics say the law is a hysterical response to a grisly crime, and relies on vague psychiatric criteria to trample on criminals' constitutional rights. The law, they add, permits the state to punish sex-crime offenders with prison, then turn around and confine them again as mentally ill. "It's a charade," says Robert Wettstein, a psychiatry professor at the University of Pittsburgh School of Medicine who has studied the law. "Washington is turning psychiatrists into jailers."

VICTIMS' RIGHTS

Backers of the predator law say it is a statute for the 1990s, reversing previous trends and putting victims' rights ahead of the the rights of criminals. Correctly administered, they say, the law is a legal "rifle shot" aimed at getting proven sex offenders off the street. Nonpredators are protected by a winnowing-out process that includes the state board, a prosecutor and a jury, supporters say. "If you use it right," says Vernon Quincey, a professor of psychology at Canada's Queens University who has reviewed the program, "it is possible to have a pretty good hit rate."

At least five other states and the city of Toronto have told Washington prosecutors they are interested in enacting similar predator laws if Washington's statute holds up in court. The state's highest court is deliberating a challenge of the law by Mr. Cunningham and another man being held; the American Civil Liberties Union has filed a brief supporting the challenge. Legal experts say the predator law is likely to end up before the U.S. Supreme Court. A decision in Washington is expected soon.

No one disputes the horror of the crime that led to the predator statute. Earl Shriner, a former convict with a 24-year history of violent sex crimes against women and children, sexually assaulted a seven-year-old Tacoma, Wash., boy and cut off his penis. While serving a previous prison term, Mr. Shriner had boasted that he intended to commit more assaults against youngsters.

LEGALLY POWERLESS

Prison officials set off a giant outcry when they admitted they knew of Mr. Shriner's plans but were legally powerless to keep him locked up after he completed his sentence. "There was enormous public concern and demands for action after that little boy was attacked," says Mr. Boerner, a former state and federal prosecutor who teaches law at the University of Puget Sound...

IN THE STATE'S GRASP

While some legislators called for new laws to do everything from mandating life sentences to castrating sex criminals, Mr. Boerner says he tried to write a law that matched the contours of the constitution but also gave the state the power to close the legal gap. His

Cartoon by Carol & Simpson. Reprinted with permission.

solution: the "mental abnormality" classification for suspected predators with a history of at least one violent sex crime. That technically made former offenders treatable, he says, and put them within the state's grasp. Washington's Legislature passed the law unanimously.

"It wouldn't have been fair if we were punishing them," Mr. Boerner says. "We're confining people for purposes of public safety and treatment, and the constitution allows that."

Others disagree. Stephen Morse, a professor of law and psychology at the University of Pennsylvania law school, says Washington "is trying to smuggle in a definition of someone not responsible for himself." In a legal brief supporting the court challenge, Washington's State Psychiatric Association calls the state's "mental abnormality" label "hopelessly vague". By basing the law on such criteria, the groups says, "the statute effectively produces a lifetime preventive detention."

Critics also say Washington's law is flawed in its belief that future violent behavior can be predicted from criminals' past sex crimes.

105

Studies of sex offenders in Massachusetts and New York show that at best such predictions will target one out of three repeaters. "You'd do better," says the University of Pennsylvania's Prof. Morse, "if you flipped a coin."

RIGHTS OF VICTIMS

But others say these criticisms miss the point of Washington's predator statute. Alexander D. Brooks, emeritus law professor at Rutgers University and an expert on the rights of the mentally ill, says that by narrowing the pool of sex criminals to those with clear histories of multiple acts of violence, officials ought to be able to pinpoint a likely group of repeaters.

More important, he says, the law reflects a shift in concern toward victims' rights. "During the last 25 years we've seen much justifiable attention paid to the rights of prisoners," he says. "But now there is growing concern for the rights of society, especially women and children who are the victims of violent sex crimes." That shift, he says, "in essence is what is being played out in Washington's sexual predator law."

For Mr. Cunningham, evidence of a shift became dramatically clear when a pair of detectives showed up as his fishing boat was preparing to leave the dock in Seattle in 1990. They slapped handcuffs on the 26-year-old former convict, hustling him off as his startled shipmates watched. Mr. Cunningham was locked up indefinitely for treatment in Washington's Special Commitment Center here — a wing of a maximum security prison.

The state has had little success in getting the men to cooperate in the treatment program so far. Only four have agreed to take part, with the rest, including Mr. Cunningham, either unwilling or still in preliminary commitment stages. William Dehmer, director of the program, says the men are offered both group and one-on-one counseling....

Victoria Roberts, chairman of the End-of-Sentence Review Committee, says the board picks candidates for predator status primarily on their past records. No members of the panel are mental health professionals. Ms. Roberts is a former prison guard. The committee calls on outside professionals for advice, she says...

"ALL DANGEROUS OFFENDERS"

"Most of our selections aren't Earl Shriners," Ms. Roberts says,

106

```
┌─────────────────────────────────────────────────────┐
│                                                       │
│              PSYCHOPATHIC PERSONALITIES               │
│                                                       │
│   Harold Monson lured boys, ages 6 to 8, into his Brooklyn │
│   Center garage with the offer of a skateboard ramp, video │
│   games, beer and pop. He sexually abused so many boys over │
│   a 17-year period, he told a psychologist, that he could not │
│   keep track of them.                                 │
│                                                       │
│   Richard Enebak of Eagan admitted raping 37 women and │
│   girls. He attacked one 16-year-old girl so viciously that she │
│   was permanently paralyzed.                          │
│                                                       │
│   Unlike most Minnesota criminals, Monson and Enebak are │
│   locked up in a hospital, not a prison. Unlike most criminals, │
│   they do not have a definite date on which they will be set free. │
│   Because their behavior is considered unstoppable, they've │
│   been declared "psychopathic personalities", and they're being │
│   held until they're considered safe to be released. Few people │
│   with psychopathic personalities are ever freed.     │
│                                                       │
│   Donna Halverson, "Sex Criminal Lockup Law Faces Challenge," St. Paul │
│   Pioneer Press, July 25, 1993                        │
│                                                       │
└─────────────────────────────────────────────────────┘
```

"but they are all dangerous offenders. Any one of them, given the opportunity, will offend again." Ms. Roberts's panel is just the first step in a three-step predator selection process that state officials say protect prisoners' rights. Step two is a review by one of the state's 39 county prosecutors. Step three is a decision by a jury, whose members are drawn from the general state juror pool.

Norman Maleng, the prosecutor whose office locked up Mr. Cunningham, disputes the ACLU's contention that the law is merely a guise for preventive detention. Ultimately, he says, the responsibility for labeling someone a sexual predator and confining him rests with a prosecutor and a jury. "We have to prove beyond a reasonable double these people have a mental abnormality that causes them to lose control of their sexual impulses," he says.

Unlike criminal juries, however, this jury doesn't have to be unanimous in deciding to civilly commit a "predator". Mr. Cunningham's 12-member jury announced it had reached its 11-to-1 decision to confine him after praying for the "wisdom of Solomon".

So far, no jury has elected to free an accused sexual predator. John La Fond, a University of Puget Sound law professor who heads the ACLU's challenge to the law, says the jury's role is subtly changed under the predator commitment procedure. By the time a suspect goes before a jury, Mr. La Fond says, his guilt has already been established, in that "the jury believes the government has already done the weeding-out process."

Whether Washington's law has curbed sexual crime isn't clear. The number of people sentenced by the state for forcible rape rose about 20% last year, and this year the total is climbing even faster. Nonetheless, says Mr. Maleng, "people feel there is a more balanced system today."

Helen Harlow agrees. The 42-year-old single mother has become a dedicated advocate for Washington's predator law and victims' rights since her son was maimed, shifting her own priorities. Before the attack she says she spent her free time campaigning for women's rights and environmental issues. "Then," she says, "God came along and said, 'Helen, here's your cause.'"

20   CONTROLLING SEXUAL OFFENDERS

TREATING SEXUAL OFFENDERS: THE POINT

Andrew Vachss

Andrew Vachss is a lawyer who represents children. He wrote this article for The New York Times.

Points to Consider:

1. Trace the psychological development of a sociopath.

2. Weigh therapy vs incarceration as a deterrent for sexual predators.

3. Respond to this statement: "Sexual predators do not outgrow their behavior."

4. Summarize the writer's recommendation for convicted sexual predators.

A Canadian survey that tracked released child molesters for 20 years revealed a 43 percent recidivism rate regardless of the therapy.

Westley Allan Dodd was hanged Tuesday morning at the Washington State Penitentiary in Walla Walla. Sentenced to execution for the torture-murder of three boys, Dodd had refused all efforts to appeal his case. He had certainly exhausted society's efforts at "rehabilitation".

A chronic, calcified sexual sadist, Dodd stated in a recent court brief, "If I do escape, I promise you I will kill and rape again and I will enjoy every minute of it." Dodd was not unique. There can be no dispute that monsters live among us. The only question is what to do with them once they become known. The death penalty is not a response. Racially and economically biased and endlessly protracted, it returns little for its enormous costs.

Though it is effective – Dodd will not strike again – the death penalty is limited to murderers; it will not protect us from rapists and child molesters who are virtually assured of release and who are almost certain to commit their crimes again. If we do not intend to execute sex criminals, does our hope lie in killing their destructive impulses?

SOCIOPATHS

People like Dodd are sociopaths. They are characterized by a fundamental lack of empathy. All children are born pure egoists. They perceive their needs to the exclusion of all others. Only through socialization do they learn that some forms of gratification must be deferred and others denied.

When a child's development is incomplete or perverted – and child abuse is the most dominant cause – he or she tends not to develop empathy. There's a missing card, one that cannot be put back in the deck once the personality is fully formed. While early childhood experiences may impel, they do not compel. In the end, evil is a matter of choice.

Sociopaths can learn to project a veneer of civilization – for predators, it is part of their camouflage – but they will always lack the ability to feel any pain but their own, pursuing only self-gratification.

110

Cartoon by David Horsey. Reprinted with special permission of North America Syndicate.

Not all sociopaths choose sexual violence. For some, the outlet can be political or economic skulduggery. But those for whom blood or pain is the stimulus act no less efficiently and at a terrible, unacceptable cost.

Some predatory sociopaths can be deterred. None can be rehabilitated because they cannot return to a state that never existed. The concept of coercive therapy is a contradiction; successful psychiatric treatment requires participants, not mere recipients. What makes sexual predators so intractable and dangerous is that, as Dodd acknowledged, they like what they do and intend to keep doing it.

TREATMENT

A 1992 study of 767 rapists and child molesters in Minnesota found those who completed psychiatric treatment were arrested more often for new sex crimes than those who had not been treated at all. A Canadian survey that tracked released child molesters for 20 years revealed a 43 percent recidivism rate regardless of the therapy.

The difference between those simply incarcerated and those subjected to a full range of treatments appears statistically negligible.

And the more violent and sadistic the offense, the more likely it is to be repeated.

Another factor that thwarts rehabilitation is the need for offenders to seek higher and higher levels of stimulation. There is no observable waning of their desires over time: sexual predators do not outgrow their behavior. Thus, while most sadistic sex offenders are not first arrested for homicide, they may well try to murder someone in the future.

What about a traditional self-help program? Should we concentrate on raising their self-esteem? Imprisoned predators receive as much fan mail as rock stars. They are courted by the news media, studied by devoted sociologists, their every word treasured as though profound. Their paintings are collected, their poetry published. Trading cards celebrate their bloody passage among us.

I recently received a letter from a young woman who gushed that, after a long exchange of letters, she was "granted visiting privileges" with Dodd and subsequently appeared on "Sally Jessy Raphael" "due to my relationship" with "Wes," who she believes is "sincere".

So do I. We simply disagree about the object of his sincerity. Sexual predators are already narcissistic; they laugh behind their masks at our attempts to understand and rehabilitate them. We have earned their contempt by our belief that they can change – by our confusion of "crazy" with "dangerous" and "sick" with "sickening".

FINAL DEFENSE

If we don't intend to execute sexual predators and we have no treatment, what is our final line of defense? There has been much discussion of voluntary castration. Such a a "remedy" ignores reality. Sexual violence is not sex gone too far; it is violence with sex as its instrument. Rage, sadism and a desire to control or debase others are the driving forces.

Castration can be reversed chemically with black-market hormones and sex murders have been committed by physically castrated rapists. People have been raped by blunt objects. And how do you castrate female offenders?

Our response to sexual predators must balance the extent and intensity of the possible behavior with the probability of its occurrence. An ex-prisoner likely to expose himself on a crowded subway may be a risk we are willing to assume. A prisoner with a moderate probability of sexual torture and murder is not.

Such violence is like a rock dropped into a calm pool – the concentric circles spread even after the rock has sunk. More and more victims will be affected. When it comes to sexual violence, the sum of our social and psychiatric knowledge adds up to this: Behavior is the truth. Chronic sexual predators have crossed an osmotic membrane. They can't step back to the other side – our side. And they don't want to. If we don't kill or release them, we have but one choice: call them monsters and isolate them.

When it comes to the sexual sadist, psychiatric diagnoses won't protect us. Appeasement endangers us. Rehabilitation is a joke. I've spoken to many predators over the years. They always exhibit amazement that we do not hunt them. And that when we capture them, we eventually let them go. Our attitude is a deliberate interference with Darwinism – an endangerment of our species.

EXPERIMENTS

A proper experiment produces answers. Experiments with sexual sadists have produced only victims. Washington State's sexual predator law will surely be challenged in the courts and it may take years before constitutional and criminological criteria are established to incarcerate a criminal beyond his or her sentence.

Perhaps no-parole life sentences for certain sex crimes would be a more straightforward answer. In any event, such laws offer our only hope against an epidemic of sexual violence that threatens to pollute our society beyond the possibility of its own rehabilitation.

21   CONTROLLING SEXUAL OFFENDERS

TREATING SEXUAL OFFENDERS: THE COUNTERPOINT

Task Force on Sexual Violence

The following was excerpted from a 1989 report issued by the Attorney General's Task Force on the Prevention of Sexual Violence Against Women for the State of Minnesota. Hubert H. Humphrey was acting Attorney General for Minnesota when this report was issued.

Points to Consider:

1. Why is mandatory treatment for sex offenders ill-advised?

2. Discuss the relationship between success in a treatment program and re-offending.

3. Analyze this recommendation: If there were only one program for sex offenders, it should be chemical dependency treatment.

4. What do successful treatment programs have in common?

Excerpted from the Minnesota Attorney General's Task Force on the Prevention of Sexual Violence Against Women, February 15, 1989.

*Treatment programs facilitate change in sex offenders'
behavior and may also provide a way to assess which
prisoners are likely to commit new offenses.*

Imposing longer sentences alone is not enough to protect women
from the threat that sex offenders will commit additional assaults.
Even with harsher sentencing guidelines and greater judicial discretion, most rapists will one day be released from prison. Treatment is
not favored by the Task Force as a benefit or right of criminals. It is
a way to increase the likelihood that offenders will change their
behavior so that they no longer threaten the safety of women when
they must be released.

Treatment programs facilitate change in sex offenders' behavior
and may also provide a way to assess which prisoners are likely to
commit new offenses. Not all sex offenders are amenable to treatment and even the most comprehensive treatment cannot guarantee
a change in behavior. The majority of the testimony heard by the
Task Force advised against mandating treatment, since the most
effective methods rely on participation in group processes and can
be undermined by an unwilling participant. Incentives for participation in treatment, however, can be provided for offenders both in
prison and on supervised release.

TREATMENT PROGRAMS

The Task Force heard testimony that current law forces judges to
choose between punishment and intensive treatment. Intensive residential treatment for a period of two or more years in duration can
be provided on probation through the Intensive Treatment Program
for Sexual Aggressives run by the Department of Human Services at
the Minnesota Security Hospital in St. Peter. Alpha House, a private
residential program in Minneapolis, also provides long-term intensive treatment for sex offenders.

The Department of Corrections has taken the initiative to provide
several different types of programming for sex offenders within an
institutional setting. The Minnesota Correctional Facility at
Stillwater provides a sex education class for offenders. Group therapy and education is provided to some 20 to 30 sex offenders in the
Special Treatment Unit at Oak Park Heights. The Transitional Sex
Offender Program (TSOP) uses 30 beds at the Lino Lakes
Correctional Facility in Stillwater. This program was established so
that sex offenders who apply, are screened for and can be accom-

JUVENILE SEX OFFENDERS

This report looks at the long-term results of a residential correctional program for juvenile sex offenders. The results for sexual re-offense are heartening; 94% of the program's released clients have not been convicted of a subsequent sexual offense.

Janis F. Bremer, "Serious Juvenile Sex Offenders," **Psychiatric Annals**, June, 1992

modated in the program can receive group therapy and supervision before sex offenders are released to the community. The Department also provides voluntary groups at the St. Cloud Correctional Facility designed for offenders whose sentences are too short to attend another program, who would like a support group after finishing another program or who have not been accepted for other treatment.

TREATING OFFENDERS

Although the Department of Corrections deserves credit for working to develop new programs for sex offenders, the Task Force heard concerns about the intensity and duration of these programs as well as concerns about the availability of space to treat all offenders assessed who need treatment. Data on the programs is limited, but both Oak Park Heights and the TSOP Program at Lino Lakes have reported that the rate of re-offending is much higher for persons who fail to complete the treatment program. After three years, 21 percent of the offenders who fail the Transitional Sex Offender Program are returned to prison on a new offense, as compared with nine percent of offenders who complete TSOP. Combining figures for new offenses and release violations, 40 percent of the offenders who fail to complete TSOP are returned to prison, as compared to 15 percent of those who complete this short-term program. This data may mean that the treatment programs effect change in behavior; it certainly means that success in a program is a factor in predicting future behavior.

Return rates may be even higher for offenders who rape as compared to those for other sex offenders. A recent State Planning Agency study shows that the rate of conviction on a new offense for violent sex offenders is approximately 21 percent, more than four

POSITIVE OUTCOMES

This past year, two articles reviewed treatment effectiveness and reported much more optimistic results. Additionally, other studies have reported positive outcomes for programs located in the community, in hospitals, and in prisons.... As diverse as they may be, successful programs do hold much in common. Today, successful programs recognize that they are part of an overall criminal justice system.

The field of sex offender treatment is growing rapidly, and more and more treatment models are being adapted for this population. The integrative model developed by the Washington Department of Corrections Sex Offender Treatment Program (but probably operating under other names in other programs) aims at responding to the individual complexity of the sex offender. It is recognized that the offender's deviance is a complex combination of physiological, cognitive, affective, social, cultural, and even spiritual issues. Not only is the problem multifaceted, but the type of technique that works best for a single individual varies widely.

Barbara K. Schwartz, "Effective Treatment Techniques for Sex Offenders," **Psychiatric Annals,** June, 1992

times the rate (5 percent) of reconviction for criminals who commit intrafamilial abuse. To evaluate the effectiveness of programs, it is important to have accurate data regarding the nature of the offense committed, participation in treatment and long-term follow up for reconviction of crime or violation of the terms of release.

Testimony also stressed that sobriety and participation in chemical dependency treatment is critical to preserve inhibitions and reduce recidivism. More than half (53 percent) of convicted sex offenders are under the influence of alcohol or other drugs while committing the sexual offense, and the percentage is steadily increasing. Alcoholics Anonymous programs are available to all inmates in Department of Corrections facilities. Correctional facilities at Stillwater, St. Cloud and Oak Park Heights also have therapeutic programming for chemical dependency treatment. One expert informed the Task Force that if he could provide only one program for sex offenders it would be chemical dependency treatment.

REENTRY OF SEX OFFENDERS INTO THE COMMUNITY

Public safety is needlessly endangered if sex offenders are released from prison to the streets without an extended program of treatment and gradual reentry into society. Many rapists require residential treatment under close observation for a year or more upon release from prison. Even where residential treatment isn't called for, long-term treatment in the community specific to sex offenders is necessary to reduce risks of re-offending. Intensive supervision is needed to monitor associations and behavior and to prevent escalation of violence before additional sexual assaults are perpetrated.

22   CONTROLLING SEXUAL OFFENDERS

AN ARGUMENT AGAINST PREVENTIVE DETENTION

Minnesota Civil Liberties Union

On Thursday, December 3, 1992, the Minnesota Civil Liberties Union (MCLU) filed an amicus curiae, *a "friend of the court" brief with the Minnesota Supreme Court in the case of* Phillip Jay Blodgett, Alleged Psychopathic Personality. *The MCLU brief contends that Minnesota's psychopathic personality statute is unconstitutional in several respects.*

Point to Consider:

1. Summarize the Minnesota psychopathic personality statute.

2. How does the Civil Liberties Union view the statute?

3. Why might the statute be perceived as a tool for preventive detention?

4. What danger is perceived in labeling a subject a "psychopathic personality"?

Excerpted from a news release by the Minnesota Civil Liberties Union, December 7, 1992. Reprinted with permission.

*Minnesota's psychopathic personality statute is a deceit-
ful and inaccurate method for the State to get around
the Constitution.*

Phillip Blodgett was convicted of two counts of felony criminal
sexual conduct in August, 1987; he had previously been convicted
of burglary in 1986, and had been found to be delinquent at the age
of 16 in 1982. He was scheduled for release from prison in
October, 1991, when the Washington County Attorney petitioned to
have Blodgett committed as a psychopathic personality. On April 2,
1992, the Washington County District Court committed Blodgett as
a psychopathic personality to the Minnesota Security Hospital at St.
Peter for an indefinite period. Blodgett appealed this order to the
Minnesota Court of Appeals on May 1, 1992. The MCLU filed an
amicus brief with the Court of Appeals contending that the psychopathic personality statute was unconstitutional.

On September 15, 1992, the Court of Appeals rejected Blodgett's
appeal, and specifically rejected the MCLU's contentions, holding
that the psychopathic personality statute did not violate either the
United States or Minnesota constitutions. Blodgett appealed to the
Minnesota Supreme Court, which accepted the case for review on
November 3, 1992.

ISSUES

The Minnesota psychopathic personality statute, enacted in 1939,
allows for the involuntary, indefinite confinement at a mental health
facility of any person meeting the statute's definition of a "psychopathic personality". That definition is:

The existence in any person of such conditions of emotional insta-
bility, or compulsiveness of behavior, or lack of customary standards of good judgment, or failure to appreciate the consequences
of his acts, or combination of any such conditions, as to render such
person irresponsible for his conduct with respect to sexual matters
and thereby dangerous to other persons.

The MCLU brief, written by volunteer attorneys John E. Grzybek
and Richard K. Ellison, contends that this statute violates the
Minnesota and Federal Constitutions in the following ways:

1. Although the statute purports to be a civil commitment statute,
it is in fact used as preventive detention; i.e., to prevent persons
from committing acts which they may or may not commit. As such,

the psychopathic personality statute is being used as punishment, without the due process of law – a trial, conviction and sentencing – required by the Fifth and Fourteenth Amendments of the United States Constitution, and by Article I, Section 7 of the Minnesota Constitution.

2. The statute is not a civil commitment statute. The concept of a "psychopathic personality" is not recognized by the medical profession. There is no treatment for such a condition; the term "psychopathic personality" on its face means that the person cannot be cured. Thus, anyone so labeled is subject to an indefinite term of imprisonment, possibly for life.

3. The statute fails to promote a state interest in public safety. The Minnesota Supreme Court has recognized the inability of psychiatrists and the lack of clinical evidence to reliably predict a person's future dangerousness. Moreover, the most current available data shows that while 175 male sex offenders were released in one year, only three percent or six offenders had returned to prison for a new sex offense one year later. The inability of the State to predict which three percent of offenders will commit a related crime again shows the indefinite and arbitrary application of the psychopathic personality statute. And, the State has other, constitutional means of accomplishing its public safety goal, such as longer sentences in the first place.

4. The statute authorizes indefinite incarceration for potential future criminal acts. In so doing it violates the constitutional requirements of due process of law by presuming guilt for uncommitted acts, and by punishing individuals for being potentially dangerous.

5. The statute permits a second sentence of incarceration on the basis of past behavior for which the individual has already been punished. As such, current use of the statute constitutes double jeopardy, in violation of the Fifth Amendment of the United States Constitution and Article I, Section 7 of the Minnesota Constitution.

6. The statute is vague and ambiguous in its language, thereby allows arbitrary enforcement, and so must be struck down under numerous United States and Minnesota Supreme Court decisions. Literally, the statute could sanction a wide range of behavior which occurs in social or intimate personal relationships.

7. Finally, in the case of Blodgett and others, further confinement

LAW CALLED UNCONSTITUTIONAL

A state law allowing sexual psychopaths to be locked up indefinitely violates their rights, an attorney argued Monday before the Minnesota Supreme Court. Phillip Blodgett is challenging his commitment to the Minnesota Security Hospital in St. Peter as a psychopathic personality.... His attorney, Richard Ilkka, said the law violates Blodgett's due process rights and should be struck down. He also said that while repeat rapists may have impaired values, they aren't mentally ill.

"Law on Sex Offenders Called Unconstitutional," **Associated Press**, March 2, 1993

through the statute violates the plea agreement entered into between the defendant and the State.

In summary, Minnesota's psychopathic personality statute is a deceitful and inaccurate method for the State to get around the Constitution, to presume guilt, to punish without trial, to punish twice for one act, to violate plea agreements, and to punish arbitrarily and indefinitely. As such the statute should be abhorrent to a free society, and should be struck down by the Minnesota Court of Appeals.

23   CONTROLLING SEXUAL OFFENDERS

IN SUPPORT OF
PREVENTIVE DETENTION

The State of Minnesota

In 1993 Philip Blodgett challenged his commitment to the Minnesota Security Hospital in St. Peter as a psychopathic personality. He was convicted of sexually assaulting two women and a teenage girl. The following article is an excerpt from a legal brief by the State of Minnesota arguing that the Minnesota Psychopathic Personalities Law did not violate the Minnesota or U.S. Constitution.

Points to Consider:

1. What are the two main options states have for dealing with convicted sexual predators?

2. Define "civil commitment statute". What is its advantage for the sex offender?

3. Summarize the intent of the Psychopathic Personality Statute.

4. What response to the Statute has been shown thus far by the U.S. Supreme Court?

Excerpted from a State of Minnesota Respondent's Brief and Addendum before the Minnesota Supreme Court, January 5, 1992.

Civil commitment of habitual sexual predators is based on the State's compelling interest in preventing more sexual assaults.

The United States Supreme Court has previously ruled that civil commitment under the psychopathic personality statute is a constitutional means of responding to the serious problem of mentally disordered, sexually predatory persons who are extremely dangerous to others...The statute applies to individuals who are distinguished by the serious nature of their disorders, the repetitive nature of their past sexual aggressions and their demonstrated inability to control their sexual impulses. In these extreme cases, it is constitutionally permissible for the State to limit the individual's liberty through civil commitment.

The psychopathic personality law was enacted on the premise that the State could protect the public while offering treatment to individuals committed by this statute. While there has been continuing debate regarding this premise, the Intensive Treatment Program for Sexual Aggressives (ITPSA) developed at the Minnesota Security Hospital has become a nationally recognized model for the treatment of sex offenders. Moreover, as explained below, there is increasing recognition in the psychiatric and medical community that treatment for disorders causing sexual aggression can be effective.

It is true that some states have simply abandoned their efforts to treat sexual predators and have repealed their "sexual psychopath" statutes. Many of these states have opted for heavy criminal penalties and more prison beds. Others, however, like the State of Washington, have recently enacted civil commitment statutes similar to Minnesota's. Use of a civil commitment statute allows the State the opportunity to protect community safety while at the same time offering something other than lifetime prison sentences, with no right to treatment or opportunity for release, for those sex offenders whose lack of control over their sexual impulses renders them exceedingly dangerous to society...

The psychopathic personality commitment statute is constitutional because it is narrowly tailored to apply only in those cases where the danger to the public is clearly identified and there are no less restrictive treatment alternatives available. Deprivation of an individual's liberty under these circumstances is not only constitutionally permissible, it is absolutely necessary in a civilized society that

Cartoon by David Seavey. Copyright 1990 **USA Today.**
Reprinted with permission.

respects the rule of law and the rights of all its citizens.

THE PSYCHOPATHIC PERSONALITY STATUTE SERVES TO CONFINE AND OFFER TREATMENT TO DANGEROUS SEXUAL OFFENDERS

It is important to consider how Minnesota's psychopathic personality law is currently being applied. The three case histories below illustrate the true psychopathology and threat to public safety which Minnesota's psychopathic personality statute is designed to address.

1. Richard Enebak.

Richard Enebak has antisocial personality disorder, which has caused him to sexually assault over 37 women and girls in the fourteen years prior to his commitment in 1970. Many of Enebak's victims sustained physical injuries in addition to the sexual assaults. In the assault which preceded his 1970 commitment, for example, Enebak fed alcohol to a 16-year-old girl until she was unconscious. Then he stripped her, violently raped her and photographed her. The pictures showed bruises around her breasts, buttocks and thighs. During the assault, the girl sustained internal injuries and several broken vertebrae, which resulted in permanent paralysis. After the assault, Enebak dumped the girl in a field with her lower body exposed. She was alive, but unable to move due to her broken vertebrae. When found, she was bleeding from severe lacerations to her vagina. When Enebak was later transferred from the Minnesota Security Hospital to an "open" hospital, he became sexually involved with a psychotic, mentally retarded patient. While on pass from the open hospital, he sexually assaulted another young girl.

2. Donald Martenies.

Donald Martenies, committed as a psychopathic personality in 1984, is diagnosed as a sexual sadist, who also has a mixed personality disorder. His long history of sexual, sadistic and aggressive behaviors began in his early childhood. Prior to his commitment, he engaged in multiple incidents of sexual abuse involving his seven-year-old stepdaughter, his nine-year-old niece, an unrelated 13-year-old girl and his wife. In addition to sexually assaulting his seven-year-old stepdaughter, he dropped her on her head on a concrete floor, hit her, put her in a freezer and pierced her calves with needles. During one of his sexual assaults on his stepdaughter, he spread her legs with such force that he ripped her perineum. He then tied her to a table and sewed her up without anesthesia. Six medical experts testified at Martenies' commitment hearing. All agreed Martenies would continue to abuse children and others unless committed to the Security Hospital.

3. Thomas Ray Duvall.

Thomas Ray Duvall is diagnosed with sexual sadism, antisocial personality and polysubstance abuse disorders. Duvall admits he is "addicted" to violent sexual interactions with young women and has acknowledged that he has no regard for the feelings or condition of his victims. His first known offense occurred at age 19 when he raped a 17-year-old girl. Three years later, he again raped another 17-year-old girl. He pled guilty to this rape and entered treatment. He left the treatment program, however, and was then sent to prison.

Duvall was paroled in 1980, but his parole was revoked after he threatened a woman with a knife and attempted to force her into his car. He returned to prison until 1982. Shortly after his release, he sexually assaulted three teen-age girls in one day. He first assaulted a 15-year-old girl on her way to school. He then assaulted two other girls aged 14 and 15, threatening one of the girls with a shotgun while he raped her. Duvall again returned to prison until 1987 when he was placed on supervised release. Within 12 days of his release, he again sexually assaulted a 17-year-old girl. This time, over a three-hour period... he threatened the victim with a knife, dragged her across the floor by her hair, tied her up with an electrical cord, wrapped her clothing around her neck, ejaculated on her face and hair, forced her to engage in oral sex, hit her with a hammer, sexually assaulted her with a curling iron or a hammer, and tied her to the bed.

THE PSYCHOPATHIC PERSONALITY STATUTE SERVES THE STATE'S COMPELLING POLICE POWER

The United States Supreme Court has recognized that states have interests which justify civil commitment under the due process clause. Civil commitment of habitual sexual predators is based on the State's compelling interest in preventing more sexual assaults on yet more innocent and vulnerable victims. The acts of sexual violence committed by psychopathic personalities are among the most heinous acts imaginable, which result in severe emotional and physical harm to their victims.

Finally, the State can offer sexual psychopaths specific treatment, which is directed to helping them gain insight into and achieve control over their sexual impulses and aggressiveness. These are all valid, compelling, rational reasons for the Legislature's decision to civilly commit only those who meet the criteria for "psychopathic personalities".

CONCLUSION

The constitutionality of the psychopathic personality law has already been upheld by both the Minnesota and the United States Supreme Courts. The law serves a legitimate and compelling state interest in protecting society in extreme cases where the danger is clearly identified and the evidence overwhelmingly establishes the need for such protection.

As the United States Supreme Court has stated, "states must be free to develop a variety of solutions" to the problems of mentally disordered and dangerous individuals. Minnesota has chosen to provide a defined class of dangerous sexual deviants security and treatment via a civil commitment process. This reasonable legislative choice must be respected.

127

WHAT IS SEX BIAS?

This activity may be used as an individualized study guide for students in libraries and resource centers or as a discussion catalyst in small group and classroom discussions.

Many readers are unaware that written material usually expresses an opinion or bias. The skill to read with insight and understanding requires the ability to detect different kinds of bias. **Political bias, race bias, sex bias, ethnocentric bias** and **religious bias** are five basic kinds of opinions expressed in editorials and literature that attempt to persuade. This activity will focus on political bias defined in the glossary below.

FIVE KINDS OF EDITORIAL OPINION OR BIAS

Sex Bias — the expression of dislike for and/or feeling of superiority over a person because of gender or sexual preference

Race Bias — the expression of dislike for and/or feeling of superiority over a racial group

Ethnocentric Bias — the expression of a belief that one's own group, race, religion, culture or nation is superior. Ethnocentric persons judge others by their own standards and values.

Political Bias — the expression of opinions and attitudes about government-related issues on the local, state, national or international level

Religious Bias — the expression of a religious belief or attitude

---

Guidelines

Read through the following statements and decide which ones represent political opinion or bias. Evaluate each statement by using the method indicated below.

- Mark (F) for any factual statements.

- Mark (S) for any statements that reflect an example of sex bias.

- Mark (O) for any statements of opinion that reflect other kinds of bias.

- Mark (N) for any statements that you are not sure about.

_____1. Many African Americans have attained freedom over the years, but to give them too much freedom will only cause problems for the nation.

_____2. Rape victims' concerns about being blamed and people finding out they had been victims, may explain why more than half of rape victims in America express concern about the news media disclosing their names.

_____3. It is more cost-effective for any given university to enroll more men than women, simply because men are more likely to succeed in school.

_____4. Genital mutilation for some is seen as a passage from childhood to adulthood. Only after they have been circumcised are the girls considered real members of society.

_____5. Jews in America always support the policies of Israel.

_____6. Tradition and technology combine today so that a woman in India is in danger from the moment she is conceived.

_____7. Poor black women are more likely to spend money on frivolous items, such as expensive clothing, cars, and jewelry.

_____8. Women's position in indigenous societies has not always been ideal; there is no reason to attempt to paint it so.

_____9. It is better to live in an all white neighborhood than a culturally mixed neighborhood, because crime is less prevalent.

_____10. Modernization and the change over to market economies have mobilized some indigenous women and left others stranded.

_____11. Most black men prefer to date white women because it provides them with more social and psychological status.

_____12. Sexually transmitted diseases are running rampant, taking a greater toll on women's lives than does AIDS in men, women and children combined.

_____13. Studies have shown that due to the superior X chromosome in the make-up of the male body, it is a scientific fact that men are more fit to survive than women.

_____14. It is a fact that women who use birth control in Mexico do so without the knowledge of their partner. This is because of the belief among men that contraceptive use makes them less of a man.

_____15. Men tend to be better mechanics than women.

_____16. Pelvic inflammatory disease is now believed to be the major preventable cause of female infertility in developing countries.

_____17. National test scores show that women are better at math than men.

_____18. According to the National Crime Report (NCR), an estimated 12.1 million American women have been the victims of forcible rape sometime in their lifetime.

_____19. Women are better at nurturing children than men.

_____20. Three of five sexual assaults occur when the victim is 17 or younger. And nearly three of 10 occur when the victim is 10 or younger.

Other Activities

1. Locate three examples of political opinion or bias in the readings from Chapter Three.

2. Make up five one-sentence statements that would each be an example of sex bias.

CHAPTER 4

INTERNATIONAL HUMAN RIGHTS
ABUSES AGAINST WOMEN

24. IN SUPPORT OF THE CONVENTION TO   132
    ELIMINATE DISCRIMINATION AGAINST
    WOMEN
    Amnesty International

25. THE CONVENTION VIOLATES THE U.S.   139
    CONSTITUTION
    Ellen Smith

26. U.S. POLICY AND GLOBAL RIGHTS FOR   144
    WOMEN: POINTS AND COUNTERPOINTS
    Jackie Wolcott vs Gordon R. Chapman

RECOGNIZING AUTHOR'S POINT OF VIEW   149
    Reasoning Skill Activity

24 INTERNATIONAL HUMAN RIGHTS ABUSES AGAINST WOMEN

IN SUPPORT OF THE CONVENTION TO ELIMINATE DISCRIMINATION AGAINST WOMEN

Amnesty International

Amnesty International is an organization devoted to stopping torture and promoting human rights world-wide.

Points to Consider:

1. Summarize the intent of the Women's Convention.

2. How many countries have ratified the Women's Convention? Has the United States?

3. List examples of human rights abuses by governments.

Excerpted from a prepared statement by Amnesty International before the U.S. Senate Foreign Relations Committee, August 2, 1990.

Amnesty International has also documented the rape of female children in detention. There are cases where children as young as three years old have been raped.

On September 18, 1979, the United Nations General Assembly adopted the Convention on the Elimination of All Forms of Discrimination Against Women (hereinafter cited as the "Women's Convention") and by September 1981, the convention entered into force. The United States signed the Women's Convention on July 17, 1980, but, despite having played a pivotal role in the drafting of the convention, has not yet ratified it. As of this date, 103 countries are state parties to the Women's Convention. The United States is, at this time, the only industrialized nation that has not ratified this international human rights treaty.

THE SUBSTANCE OF THE WOMEN'S CONVENTION

The Women's Convention provides the world community with an international framework of standards for the recognition and protection of women's rights as human rights. The Women's Convention is a comprehensive codification of the right to nondiscrimination on the basis of gender. The convention defines discrimination against women as "any distinction, exclusion, or restriction based on sex, that has the effect or purpose of impairing or nullifying the recognition, enjoyment, or exercise by women of human rights and fundamental freedoms." The convention calls upon all state parties to take appropriate measures in all fields to ensure the full development and advancement of women, for the purpose of guaranteeing them the exercise and enjoyment of human rights and fundamental freedoms on the basis of equality with men...

HUMAN RIGHTS ABUSES

Amnesty International finds the Women's Convention relevant to its concerns. Article 3 of the convention prohibits all activities that violate women's human rights and calls upon the respective states parties to undertake measures to ensure that women's human rights are protected and promoted.

Amnesty International has documented myriad cases of abuses of men and women by government officials and found that women in custody may be more likely to face gender-specific violations of human rights, such as rape, sexual assault, and sexual intimidation. Women in vulnerable situations are often the victims of governmental abuse. There are numerous cases of pregnant women who upon being detained are tortured and face prison conditions that amount to cruel, inhuman, and degrading treatment. Some pregnant women are denied the most basic medical care and as a result they frequently miscarry.

In some cases, women are threatened with harm to their children, or the children are used to force the mothers to make a statement. Yet other Amnesty cases indicate the practice of torture against women as a way of threatening the community or putting pressure on a male relative or friend. In many countries, women are detained, tortured, or even killed because of their association with a male counterpart.

These abuses occur in countries all over the world. The victims of these abuses are women of all ages, from all walks of life: agricultural workers, journalists, trade unionists, physicians, lawyers, students, homemakers, political activists, religious and community workers. They may be targeted by their governments for their beliefs, religion, political activity, race, nationality, or ethnic origin and once detained, are often subjected to violence. . .

RAPE AND SEXUAL ABUSE

The rape of women and female children in custody by law enforcement officials is an intentional infliction of pain and suffering, both physical and mental. As such, it is a form of torture and clearly prohibited by international standards. Amnesty International USA is concerned that rape and sexual abuse in custody occur more frequently than our reports indicate. Many women do not report such abuses because of humiliation or fear of further assaults.

Rape and sexual abuse occur in women's homes, during the process of searches, arrest, and interrogation and while in detention by police, soldiers, guards, or others acting with official acquiescence. Amnesty has noted cases of rape used as a reprisal by governmental entities against a local community. Amnesty is concerned by the refusal of government officials to investigate and prosecute local authorities who rape women in custody.

Maria Juana Medina was detained in El Salvador on Sept. 18, 1989, along with 63 others during mass arrests following a demonstration by the trade union federation FENASTRAS in El Salvador. Maria Juana Medina stated in a testimony to a Salvadoran human

322 EIGHTH AVENUE NEW YORK, NEW YORK 10001

rights organization that during her detention, she was raped and repeatedly kicked in the abdomen, causing severe inflammation. She was hung by her feet over a stairwell and threatened with immersion in an electrified pool and with having her teeth pulled out if she did not confess to being a member of the FMLN. She denied the accusations, explaining that she had spent about a month in the FENASTRAS offices investigating the whereabouts of her daughter, who had "disappeared". She was examined on the third day of her detention by somebody who appeared to be a doctor, who recommended that she be taken to a hospital immediately. The police refused, stating that this would reveal that they had used torture...

CHILDREN RAPED IN CUSTODY

Amnesty International has also documented the rape of female children in detention. There are cases where children as young as three years old have been raped. Iris Yomila Reyes Urizar, the 15-year-old niece of a Guatemalan human rights activist, was reported raped in custody of the armed forces in February 1989. The girl escaped her captors and family members denounced the incident to the justice of the peace who ordered her examined by a forensic doctor. The doctor confirmed that the girl had been raped. In

135

Turkey, 16-year-old Saadet Akkaya was arrested in April 1988. She testified that she was tortured by being hung from a cross and given electric shocks on her fingertips and nipples and then sexually assaulted. On the order of one policeman, she was then removed from the cross and raped by another policeman.

Girls are vulnerable both as females and as children and should be entitled to additional protection. It is essential that additional measures be taken to guard against these abuses. It is essential that allegations of rape be examined seriously by authorities and that the perpetrators be brought to justice. . .

PREGNANCY, HEALTH CARE, AND CHILDBIRTH IN DETENTION

Article 12 of the Women's Convention calls on government to ensure appropriate medical services in connection with pregnancy, confinement, and the postnatal period. In addition, the U.N. Standard Minimum Rules for the Treatment of Prisoners requires that special accommodations be made for all necessary prenatal and postnatal care and treatment. In many countries, pregnant prisoners are tortured, ill-treated, and denied adequate nourishment and medical attention which in many cases leads to miscarriage and permanent physical damage.

Debra Marakalla, a human rights activist in South Africa, received no medical attention while hemorrhaging in her cell and was taken to hospital after the miscarriage had already occurred. In El Salvador, Morena Margarita Rivas Quijada, a 25-year-old secretary and student, was recently arrested when she was three months pregnant. According to her testimony, she was tortured, forced to stand for days with her hands tied over her head, and continually threatened with rape. Her health deteriorated in prison and she gave birth after six months to a tiny infant who died a few weeks after birth.

Teresa del Rosario-Castro Caceres, a housekeeper for the staff of the Lutheran World Federation in San Salvador was detained on November 30, 1989. She was held for days at the headquarters of the Treasury Police, where she was raped and beaten. She was two months pregnant at the time of her detention and suffered a miscarriage as a result of the torture.

In Somalia, Amnesty has documented several cases of women political detainees who gave birth in prison with little or no medical

136

attention. Their newborn infants were taken from them only a few hours after birth and they did not hear of their fate for years afterward. Safia Hashi Madar, a relief worker, was arrested when she was nine months pregnant and denied prenatal and postnatal medical treatment. As a result of the combination of torture and the lack of medical attention in the late pregnancy period, she suffered severe kidney infection, malnourishment, and gynecological complications. The authorities refused to give her any medical treatment or to allow her family to provide it.

Teenage mothers of newborn babies in Brazilian jails suffer yet another form of cruelty to themselves which also endangers the lives of their newborn children. The babies are purposely taken away from the nursing mothers with the intention of causing prolonged pain to the mothers. In Iran, babies have been taken from their mothers and denied milk. Their screams caused the mothers mental anguish as well as physical pain.

In other cases, children suffer severe physical damage due to ill health and lack of medical care in prison. In Ethiopia, Namat Issa was arrested in 1980 when she was seven months pregnant. She gave birth to a son, Amonsissa, in prison. Her son caught a virus infection in 1983, possibly cerebral meningitis, which went untreated and resulted in brain damage and mental retardation...

CONCLUSION

These are but a few examples of the issues and cases of concern to Amnesty International which are addressed by the Women's

Convention. Amnesty International works to promote human rights through adherence of states to international human rights treaties. The Women's Convention is an important instrument of international law as it provides a framework for defining and promoting women's rights as well as a means to eradicate discriminatory practices or laws that violate the human rights and fundamental freedoms of women.

25   INTERNATIONAL HUMAN RIGHTS ABUSES AGAINST WOMEN

THE CONVENTION VIOLATES THE U.S. CONSTITUTION

Ellen Smith

Ellen Smith wrote the following comments as a representative of concerned Women for America, an organization representing over 700,000 members around the nation whose stated purpose is to defend the "timeless legal and moral values" of the "traditional American family".

Points to Consider:

1. Summarize the provisions of the Equal Protection Clause of the 14th Amendment and the Due Process Clause of the 5th Amendment as they relate to women's equality.

2. How does the Women's Convention definition of discrimination go beyond American Law?

3. Give example of Convention articles that Smith regards as "radically feminist" and "anti-family".

4. Comment on the following statement: "The Convention would trample upon individual liberties."

Excerpted from testimony by Ellen Smith before the U.S. Senate Foreign Relations Committee, August 2, 1990.

This Convention is not about the elimination of "discrimination" against women or the protection of fundamental human rights.

Mr. Chairman, thank you for this opportunity to meet with you and your colleagues of the Foreign Relations Committee to address the Convention on the Elimination of All Forms of Discrimination Against Women. In my testimony today, I am addressing the document as a whole and will not offer specific recommendations as to the adoption of Reservations to the Convention.

I am here this morning on behalf of Concerned Women for America, an organization representing over 700,000 members around the nation. Our stated purpose is to preserve and defend the timeless legal and moral values upon which our nation was founded and the rights of the traditional American family. The Convention presently being considered raises a number of issues of concern for our organization and our constituents.

THE SUPREME COURT

The United States Supreme Court has applied the Equal Protection Clause of the 14th Amendment and the Due Process Clause of the 5th Amendment to invalidate state and federal laws requiring disparate treatment of "similarly situated" men and women. This understanding provides reasonable flexibility by allowing for common sense distinctions that serve important governmental objectives. In addition, current state and federal statutes prohibit discrimination against women in employment, housing, education, credit, immigration and a number of other areas. Concerned Women for America has consistently supported the firmly rooted principle in American jurisprudence of equality under the law.

Were this Convention limited to these basic, legitimate concerns for constitutional and civil liberty, our objection would be less strenuous. However, the Convention assumes a definition of discrimination that is of astonishing breadth and goes far beyond the understanding of discrimination as it has been addressed in American law. The document defines "discrimination" as "any distinction, exclusion or restriction made on the basis of sex which has the effect or purpose of impairing or nullifying the recognition, enjoyment or exercise by women..." of their rights. Furthermore, the Convention is applicable not only to governmental actions/policies, but to private associations and organizations and even to private

U.N. WOMEN DISCRIMINATION TREATY

It would be a very bad idea to resurrect this treaty from the dustbin of history. It would grievously interfere with our constitutional federal-state balance of powers, overturn or change many of our current laws, and bring international regulation into areas that constitutionally are reserved to state, local or private discretion.

The U.N. treaty may be good for other countries where women do not enjoy the rights that American women take for granted. But it would be an embarrassment for the U.S. Senate to ratify it because it is so contrary to American institutions, culture, traditions, Constitution and relationships.

Phylis Schlafly, "U.N. Women Discrimination Treaty," **Human Events**, September 15, 1990

individuals in the scope of their thoughts, customs and interpersonal interactions.

The result, or perhaps the objective, of adopting such a comprehensive definition, is to demand, by logical extension, policies having the de facto effect of eliminating not only common sense distinctions between men and women, but of eliminating their situational differences in virtually every sphere of human endeavor.

Whether or not the treaty is self-executing is at best unclear, although the Convention calls for "appropriate measures" to implement its provisions. Even if the provisions cannot be judicially enforced apart from implementing legislation, the understanding of "human rights" as articulated in the convention is by no means universally accepted in this country as embodying wise or prudent public policy, much less as embodying fundamental "human rights".

SOCIAL PLANNING

This Convention is not about the elimination of "discrimination" against women or the protection of fundamental human rights. Rather, the drafters have used the rhetoric of "women's rights" to advance a vision of society which presupposes the propriety of extensive economic and social planning. Ironically, while the nations of Eastern Europe are hurriedly rejecting these presuppositions, the U.S. Senate is being wooed to accept such bankrupt policies as embodied in this document.

Many articles of the Convention read like a laundry list of radically feminist, anti-family policy objectives that have failed to gain acceptance as domestic policy initiatives. For example, Article 11 envisions extensive government intervention into the private sector: government wage-setting through comparable worth programs, government child care and government determination of employee benefits such as "paid leave".

The Convention also attempts to break down the natural walls defining and distinguishing the jurisdictions of individual, family, and society. Perhaps the most brazen example is found in Article 5, Section (b) regarding "family education", implying that families should be taught the politically proper fashion in which to arrange their private affairs and train their children. Motherhood is mechanistically defined as a "social function", conjuring up images of women bearing children out of service to society. Furthermore, civil libertarian concerns are raised by Article 5, Section (a), referring to measures to "modify" social and cultural patterns, and Article 10, effectively calling for government censorship of textbooks to purge them of unapproved ideas. The Convention does not appear to restrict this provision to public education.

PRIMARY CONCERNS

One of the primary concerns raised during the debates over the Equal Rights Amendment was that its innocuous sounding language was so vague as to allow for unspecified and ill-defined ramifications. A number of key provisions in this Convention raise similar concerns. For instance, Articles 14 and 16 address a number of family planning issues, including the right to determine the "number and spacing of children" as well as the right to "access to the information, education and means to enable" the exercise of those "rights". This language could quite reasonably be construed to mandate public financing of abortion, on demand, with no restrictions whatsoever. The American people have issued no such mandate.

Contrary to what you may hear from the proponents of this agenda, these initiatives do not necessarily reflect or represent the views and convictions of the majority of American women. In effect, they constitute "ERA" on an international scale, abortion on demand, and numerous other controversial policies that have been rejected by the American people and by our duly-elected representatives in this republic. In addition, the Convention would trample upon individual liberties, the Judeo-Christian model of the family, and our national sovereignty. Without qualifying reservations, the Convention violates Constitutional and historical principles of federalism by dictating policy in areas such as education and domestic relations, heretofore deemed among those powers retained by the states. Furthermore, if indeed the Convention is self-executing, it circumvents, in heavy-handed fashion, the normal legislative process as it relates to domestic policy.

Article 24 of the Convention obligates the States Parties to "undertake to adopt all necessary measures at the national level aimed at achieving the full realization of the rights recognized in the present Convention." On the most fundamental level, we object to the Convention's definition of discrimination and its characterization of these so-called "rights". In fact, by equating rights with particular and controversial political objectives, the Convention trivializes the very notion of human rights, or, in the language of the Declaration of Independence, the "unalienable rights" endowed by the Creator. We are convinced that the most pro-family, pro-women policy this body can pursue is one that continues to protect legal equality of opportunity, as already secured by the Constitution and statutes of this nation.

26   INTERNATIONAL HUMAN RIGHTS ABUSES AGAINST WOMEN

U.S. POLICY AND GLOBAL RIGHTS FOR WOMEN: Points & Counterpoints

Jackie Wolcott vs Gordon R. Chapman

Jackie Wolcott wrote the following comments in her capacity as the Deputy Assistant Secretary for International Social and Humanitarian Affairs in the Bureau of International Organizational Affairs at the Department of State. Gordon R. Chapman submitted the following statement to the Committee on Foreign Relations of the House of Representatives.

Points to Consider:

1. Briefly summarize measures the United States has taken to promote human rights for women.

2. What is CEDAW and when was it enacted by the General Assembly?

3. According to Chapman, what is "the bottom line for international law"? Has the U.S. supported decisions by the World Court?

4. Analyze: "There is undoubtedly a serious public misunderstanding that the U.S. strongly supports the U.N."

Excerpted from testimony by Jackie Wolcott and Gordon R. Chapman before the U.S. House Foreign Affairs Committee, Subcommittee on Human Rights, March 21 and July 26, 1990.

The Point

Jackie Wolcott

I would like to outline what measures the Department of State has taken to promote the human rights of women worldwide. I will also outline some of the measures the United States Government has pursued in the United Nations in order to advance the status of women. . . This Administration is committed to promoting and protecting human rights of all individuals. We are particularly concerned about the rights of women.

The United States has been an active member of the United Nations Commission on the Status of Women since it was established in 1946. At the most recent session of the Commission, we introduced, promoted, and co-sponsored resolutions not only to eradicate violence against women but also to advance the status and to improve the lives of women worldwide.

COMMUNICATIONS CONCERNING THE STATUS OF WOMEN

At the 34th Session of the Commission on the Status of Women, the United States introduced a resolution on communications concerning the status of women. The "communications" procedure allows individuals and non-governmental organizations to file complaints of gender discrimination by governments.

We envision that, as this procedure receives greater publicity and use, it will be an impetus for governments to take positive steps to eradicate violence and abuse against women and to remove barriers to women's full participation in their societies.

PHYSICAL VIOLENCE AGAINST DETAINED WOMEN

At the 34th Session of the U.N. Commission on the Status of Women, the U.S. co-sponsored a resolution on physical violence against detained women that is specific to their sex. It called upon Member States to take appropriate measures to eradicate these acts of violence and to report to the Secretary-General on legislative and other measures they have taken to prevent such violence. The Department of State will work with the Department of Justice in reporting on what the United States has done to eradicate acts of violence against detained women.

REFUGEE WOMEN

The United States is greatly concerned about the condition of refugee women and children, who account for eighty percent of the refugee population. Refugee and displaced women are sometimes harassed and intimidated by male guards and camp officials. They are also largely excluded from decision-making that affects their lives. The United States strongly supports international efforts to involve women refugees in this decision-making process, and to increase the number of women employed by U.N. refugee assistance agencies. . .

CEDAW

The Senate may soon be concluding its consideration of the Torture Convention. Both the Administration and the Senate had identified this Convention as a priority, and we hope that the Senate will soon provide its advice and consent to ratification.

Once we obtain Senate advice and consent to ratification of the Torture Convention, the Administration looks forward to working with both Houses of Congress to determine which of the other human rights treaties should be considered. The Convention on the Elimination of All Forms of Discrimination Against Women (CEDAW) is certainly a candidate. Other pending conventions include the International Covenant on Civil and Political Rights, the Convention on the Elimination of All Forms of Racial Discrimination, and the Convention on the Rights of the Child.

In light of Congressional interest in CEDAW, the Department of State has requested the Department of Justice to review the Convention to determine whether any of its provisions conflict with current U.S. law.

The Counterpoint

Gordon R. Chapman

I have provided for this committee 44 instruments of international law — Agreements, Covenants, Conventions, and Protocols — and 16 Declarations passed by the General Assembly dealing with Human Rights. All of the instruments deal directly or indirectly with the victimization, discrimination, or rights and status of women and children. They include those passed and ratified by the League of

Nations and updated by the United Nations...

The body of U.N. instruments listed for this committee includes those most relevant to reducing discrimination and violence against women and children and improving their social, legal, and economic status. The body of international law that it forms is still very weak despite the strong language in which most of the instruments are worded. Implementation is the weakest aspect of the instruments, because of the paucity of measures provided by Member States individually or through the U.N. budget and agency programs. Few of the Member States are willing to wholeheartedly engage in and support international human rights activities without substantial redefinition of terms and conditions to meet local social, cultural, and political criteria. The bottom line for international law, as for national and local law, is the court. Anything short of that is based on moral suasion, agreement, and convenience. But only 51 countries have subscribed to the World Court by signing the required declaration to abide by its rulings.

THE UNITED STATES

The U.S. is an important case in point. The U.S. government has not subscribed to the World Court, nor to most of the human rights conventions listed here. There is undoubtedly a serious public misunderstanding that the U.S. strongly supports the U.N. and the work of the U.N. to implement the principles of its charter. This may be because the Charter was signed in San Francisco, because the Roosevelt, Truman, and Eisenhower administrations supported the U.N. strongly, because of the efforts of Eleanor Roosevelt and Adlai Stevenson in the area of human rights, and because the headquarters of the U.N. was established in New York, and other reasons as well.

However, examination of the positions that the U.S. has taken on the human rights instruments belies that claim. Of the 44 instruments listed here, the U.S. has ratified 13, signed without ratifying 9, and has taken no action on 22. For example, the U.S. has not signed or ratified agreements or conventions dealing with the suppression of slavery, torture and other cruel, inhuman or degrading treatment or punishment; traffic in women and children; traffic in obscene publications; discrimination in education and employment; human rights (covenants), elimination of discrimination against women, and for the rights of the child. (The U.S. voting record in the General Assembly on the 16 declarations dealing with Human

147

Rights was not checked for this listing.) Obviously, further analysis should be carried out on the circumstances and subtleties in the U.S. human rights positions, but a simple examination of the list indicates U.S. positions that are at least not very supportive of efforts to implement the Charter.

AN ENIGMA

U.S. positions must seem an enigma to other countries in view of the importance given human rights in the U.S., the numerous statements made about international human rights at all levels of government, and the role of human rights in U.S. foreign policy historically. For the past several years, efforts have been growing to get the U.S. Senate to ratify the Convention on the Elimination of All Forms of Discrimination Against Women, which the General Assembly enacted in 1979. To that effort must be added a new effort to get the President to sign and the Senate to ratify the Convention on the Rights of the Child. Both of these conventions are more comprehensive than past instruments in that they bring together the subjects of earlier instruments. They also provide broader and more extensive mechanisms for monitoring, analyzing, reporting and dealing with violations.

RECOGNIZING AUTHOR'S POINT OF VIEW

This activity may be used as an individualized study guide for students in libraries and resource centers or as a discussion catalyst in small group and classroom discussions.

Many readers are unaware that written material usually expresses an opinion or bias. The capacity to recognize an author's point of view is an essential reading skill. The skill to read with insight and understanding involves the ability to detect different kinds of opinions or bias. **Sex bias, race bias, ethnocentric bias, political bias** and **religious bias** are five basic kinds of opinions expressed in editorials and all literature that attempts to persude. They are briefly defined in the glossary below.

FIVE KINDS OF EDITORIAL OPINION OR BIAS

Sex Bias — the expression of dislike for and/or feeling of superiority over the opposite sex or a particular sexual minority

Race Bias — the expression of dislike for and/or feeling of superiority over a racial group

Ethnocentric Bias — the expression of a belief that one's own group, race, religion, culture or nation is superior. Ethnocentric persons judge others by their own standards and values.

Political Bias — the expression of political opinions and attitudes about domestic or foreign affairs

Religious Bias — the expression of a religious belief or attitude

---

Guidelines

1. Locate three examples of political opinion or bias in the readings

from Chapter Four.

2. Locate five sentences that provide examples of any kind of editorial opinion or bias from the readings in Chapter Four.

3. Write down each of the above sentences and determine what kind of bias each sentence represents. Is it **sex bias, race bias, ethnocentric bias, political bias** or **religious bias?**

4. Make up one-sentence statements that would be an example of each of the following: **sex bias, race bias, ethnocentric bias, political bias** and **religious bias.**

5. See if you can locate five sentences that are factual statements from the readings in Chapter Four.

Summarize author's point of view in one sentence for each of the following readings:

Reading 19_____

Reading 20_____

Reading 21_____

Reading 22_____

Reading 23_____

Reading 24_____

Reading 25_____

Reading 26_____

BIBLIOGRAPHY

General References

Chatterjee, Mirai. "Women Taking Control, Remaking India's Economy." **Multinational Monitor** Nov. 1991: 16-8.

"Japan Textbooks to Tell About WWII Sex Slaves." **Star Tribune**, Minneapolis, 2 July 1993: n.p.

Katz, Gregory. "Mexican City Where Women Hold Power Sanctuary from Rape, Assault." **Saint Paul Pioneer Press** 7 June 1993: 1A, 4A.

Piccolino, Alberta. "Brazilian Women Battle Enormous Odds in Reproductive Rights Snarl." **National Catholic Reporter** 20 Dec. 1991: 11.

Rodrigue, George. "Swedes Revolutionize Fight Against Violence." **Dallas Morning News** 15 May 1993: n.p.

"War's Rape Victims Have Nowhere to Turn in Croatia." **Los Angeles Times** 5 Dec. 1992: n.p.

Domestic Violence

"Battered Women: Why Do They Stay?" **Psychology Today** May/June 1992: 22.

Elshtain, J.B. "Battered Reason." **The New Republic** 5 Oct. 1992: 25+.

Hopkins, E. "Nowhere to Run." **Rolling Stone** 11 June 1992: 169+.

"Men of Mean." **Psychology Today** Sept./Oct. 1992: 18.

Shottenkirk, D. "Making Domestic Violence Public." **Ms.** May/June 1992: 77.

Rape

Cockburn, A. "The Lynching of Paulinho Paiakan." **The Nation** 28 Sept. 1992: 314-315+.

Cockburn, A. "Rainforest Crunch." **The Nation** 30 Nov. 1992: 650+.

Corliss, R. "The Jock as Fallen Idol." **Time** 6 Apr. 1992: 60.

Foote, J. "Ireland's Abortion Anguish." **Newsweek** 2 Mar. 1992: 48.

Freed, L. "Locked In." **The New York Times Magazine** 22 Mar. 1992: 22+.

Gilbert, N. "Realities and Mythologies of Rape." **Society** May/June 1992: 4-10.

Gill, J.F. "Heroes Take a Fall." **The New York Times Magazine** 30 Aug. 1992: 14+.

"The Horror of Rape in America." **Star Tribune,** Minneapolis 24 Apr. 1992: 1A, 11A.

"In Texas, a Grim Question of Survival: An Accused Rapist Insists an Offered Condom Implied Consent." **Time** 9 Nov. 1992: 26.

"Ireland's Abortion Controversy." **World Press Review** Apr. 1992: 8.

Kaminker, L. "An Angry Cry for Mute Voices." **Newsweek** 16 Nov. 1992: 16.

Kass, L. "Daughters and Sisters." **Commentary** July 1992: 10-13.

Kass, L. "Regarding Daughter and Sisters: The Rape of Dinah." **Commentary** Apr. 1992: 29-38.

Klein, Marty. "Stopping Rape: Women, Read This to Men." **Utne Reader** Nov./Dec. 1988: 109-11.

Knight, R. "A Very Deep Crisis." **U.S. News & World Report** 2 Mar. 1992: 24.

Lacayo, R. "Sentences Inscribed on Flesh." **Time** 23 Mar. 1992: 54+.

"Make Mass Rape a War Crime, U.N. Urged." **The Christian Century** 28 Apr. 1992: 448-9.

Matulis, S. "Why Abortioin Must Remain the Law of the Land." **The Humanist** July/Aug. 1992: 35-7+.

Meyer, M.R. "Coercing Sex Behind Bars." **Newsweek** 9 Nov. 1992: 76-8.

Nixon, A.A. "Against All Odds." **Reader's Digest** Mar. 1992: 104-8.

Oates, J.C. "Rape and the Boxing Ring." **Newsweek** 24 Feb. 1992: 60-1.

Pooley, E. "Why Are These Guys Laughing?" **New York** 13 Apr. 1992: 58-63.

"Race and Rape." **The Nation** 8 Oct. 1990: 368-9.

"Rape Study: Only 16% Are Reported." **Star Tribune,** Minneapolis 24 Apr. 1992: 1A, 11A.

Robinson, M. "Unveiled." **The New Republic** 9 Mar. 1992: 11-2.

A Round-up of Rapists." **Psychology Today** Nov./Dec. 1992: 12-3.

Scully, D. "Who's to Blame for Sexual Violence?" **USA Today** Jan. 1992: 35-7.

Serrill, M.S. "A Case of Blind Justice." **Time** 2 Mar. 1992: 33.

Smith, Barbara. "Jogger Rape: Ask a Black Feminist." **Guardian** 7 Nov. 1990: 18.

Tarshis, L. "The War on Women." **Scholastic Update** 3 Apr. 1992: 14-6.

"Unsettling Report on an Epidemic of Rape." **Time** 4 May 1992: 15.

Van den Haag, E. "Thinking About Rape." **The American Spectator**. Apr. 1992: 56-7.

Scholarly References

Balcom, Dennis. "Shame and Violence: Consideration in Couples' Treatment." **Journal of Independent Social Work** 1991: 5, 3-4, 165-181.

Berliner, Lucy, and Mary P. Koss. "Facts of Advocacy Statistics: The Case of Acquaintance Rape." **Journal of Interpersonal Violence** Mar. 1992: 7, 1, 121-122.

Bingham, Shereen G. "Communication Strategies for Managing Sexual Harassment in Organizations: Understanding Message Options and Their Effects." **Journal of Applied Communication Research** June 1991: 19, 1-2, 88-115.

Bremer, Barbara A.; Cathleen T. Moore.; and Ellen F. Bildersee. "Do You Have to Call It 'Sexual Harassment' to Feel Harassed?" **College Student Journal** Sept. 1991: 25, 3, 258-268.

Brush, Lisa D. "Violent Acts and Injurious Outcomes in Married Couples: Methodological Issues in the National Survey of Families and Households." **Gender and Society** Mar. 1990: 4, 1, 56-67.

Bunch, Charlotte. "Recognizing Women's Rights as Human Rights." **Response to the Victimization of Women and Children** Winter, 1990: 13, 4, 13-16.

Cohen, Lloyd R. "Sexual Harassment and the Law." **Society** May-June 1991: 28, 4(192), 8-13.

Costa, Luann; and Debra Holliday. "Considerations for the Treatment of Marital Violence." **Journal of Mental Health Counseling** Jan. 1993: v. 15, n. 1, 26-36.

Crossman, Rita K.; Stith, Sandra M.; and Bender, Mary M. "Sex Role Egalitarianism and Marital Violence." **Sex Roles** Mar. 1990: 22, 5-6, 293-304.

Dervin, Dan. "Testimony of Silence: A Psychohistorical Perspective on the Thomas-Hill Hearings." **Journal of Psychohistory** Winter 1992: 19, 3, 257-268.

Dewhurst, Ann Marie, and Others. "Aggression Against Women by Men: Sexual and Spousal Assault." **Journal of Offender Rehabilitation** 1992: v. 18, n. 3-4, 39-47.

Dobash, Russell P.; R. Emerson Dobash.; Margo Wilson.; and Martin Daly. "The Myth of Sexual Symmetry in Marital Violence." **Social Problems** Feb. 1992: 39, 1, 71-91.

Gondolf, Edward W. "The Human Rights of Women Survivors." **Response to the Victimization of Women and Children,** Summer 1990: 13, 2, 6-8.

Greene, Edith; Allan Raitz.; and Heidi Lindblad. "Jurors' Knowledge of Battered Women." **Journal of Family Violence** June 1989: 4, 2, 105-125.

Gruber, James E. "A Typology of Personal and Environmental Sexual Harassment: Research and Policy Implications for the 1990s." **Sex Roles** June 1992: 26, 11-12, 447-464.

Gwartney-Gibbs, Patricia A.; and Denise H. Lach. "Sociological Explanations for Failure to Seek Sexual Harassment Remedies." **Mediation Quarterly** Summer 1992: 9, 4, 363-374.

Jaschik, Mollie L.; and Bruce R. Fretz. "Women's Perceptions and Labeling of Sexual Harassment." **Sex Roles** July 1992: 25, 19-23.

Jones, Tricia S; and Martin S. Remland. "Sources of Variability in Perceptions of and Responses to Sexual Harassment." **Sex Roles** Aug. 1992: 27-, 3-4, 121-142.

Kaplan, Sally J. "Consequences of Sexual Harassment in the Workplace." **Affilia** Fall 1991: 6, 3, 50-65.

Kilgour, David. "Ending Violence Against Women." **Canadian Social Studies** Summer 1992: v. 26, n. 4, 142-43.

Kissling, Elizabeth Arveda. "Street Harassment: The Language of Sexual Terrorism." **Discourse and Society** Oct. 1992: 2, 4, 451-460.

Mann, Cynthia A.; Michael L. Hecht; and Kristin B. Valentine. "Performance in a Social Context: Date Rape Versus Date Right." **Central States Speech Journal** Fall-Winter 1988: 39, 3-4, 269-280.

McKinney, Kathleen; and Kelly Crittenden. "Contrapower Sexual Harassment: The Offender's Viewpoint." **Free Inquiry in Creative Sociology** May 1992: 20, 1, 3-10.

Niebuhr, Robert E.; and Wiley R. Boyles. "Sexual Harassment of Military Personnel: An Examination of Power Differentials." **International Journal of Intercultural Relations** 1991: 15, 4, 445-457.

Rosenbaum, Alan. "Methodological Issues in Marital Violence Research." **Journal of Family Violence** June 1988: 3,, 2, 91-104.

Patterson, Orlando; and G.B. Teeple. "Race, Gender and Liberal Fallacies." **Society-Societe** Feb. 1992: 16, 1, 1-4.

Peterson, Steven A.; and Bettina Franzese. "Correlates of College Men's Sexual Abuse of Women." **Journal of College Student Personnel** May 1987: v. 28, n. 3, 223-28.

Pineau, Lois. "Date Rape: A Feminist Analysis." **Law and Philosophy** Aug. 1989: 8, 2, 217-243.

Reilly, Mary Ellen; Bernice Lott; Donna Caldwell; and Luisa DeLuca. "Tolerance for Sexual Harassment Related to Self-Reported Sexual Victimization." **Gender and Society** Mar. 1992: 6, 1, 122-138.

Schneider, Beth E. "Put Up and Shut Up: Workplace Sexual Assaults." **Gender and Society** Dec. 1991: 5, 4, 533-548.

Schwartz, Martin D. "Humanist Sociology and Date Rape on the College Campus." **Humanity and Society** Aug. 1991: 15, 3, 304-316.

Shrier, Diane K. "Sexual Harassment and Discrimination: Impact on Physical and Mental Health." **New Jersey Medicine** Feb. 1990: 87, 2, 105-107.

Shotland, R. Lance. "A Theory of the Causes of Courtship Rape: Part 2." **Journal of Social Issues** Spring 1992: 48, 127-143.

Stith, Sandra M. "Police Response to Domestic Violence: The Influence of Individual and Familial Factors." **Violence and Victims** Spring 1990: 5, 1, 37-49.

Stone, Deborah A. "Race, Gender, and the Supreme Court." **American Prospect** Winter 1992: 8, 63-73.

Thomas, Dorothy Q.; and Michele E. Beasley. "Domestic Violence as a Human Rights Issue." **Human Rights Quarterly** Feb. 1993: 15, 1, 36-62.

Williams, Karen B.; and Ramona R. Cyr. "Escalating Commitment to a Relationship: The Sexual Harassment Trap." **Sex Roles** July 1992: 27, 1-2, 47-72.

Williams, Kirk R. "Social Sources of Marital Violence and Deterrence: Testing an Integrated Theory of Assaults between Partners." **Journal of Marriage and the Family** Aug. 1992: v. 54, n. 3, 620-29.

Williams, Kirk R.; and Richard Hawkins. "Wife Assault, Costs of Arrest, and the Deterrence Process." **Journal of Research in Crime and Delinquency** Aug. 1992: 29, 3, 292-310.